"If you are grieving over a lost child right now, as are most of the parents who write me, these words are for you to put up in a prominent place, to remember them as daily exhortations:

God Didn't Promise We'd Be Leading at the Half,
but Only That We Would Win the Game!

You can recover and gain confidence for your children by remembering that loving your child is a long-term investment, not a short-term loan."

Fresh Elastic for Stretched Out Moms is for all parents whose hearts have been broken by their children. Barbara Johnson understands the hopelessness that you experience when your children choose rebellious lifestyles, commit suicide, or severely hurt you in some other manner. She walks you slowly and gently through a revitalizing program to a fresh, hope-filled start. She allows her love and compassion to wash over you and heal you. You'll capture her infectious enthusiasm for living through the rib-tickling anecdotes, heartwarming poetry, and poignant recollections she shares throughout this hope-filled joyous book. You'll also find transforming principles that will enable you to look upon each day as a "new beginning" and trust God to give you victory over depression and despair. *Fresh Elastic for Stretched Out Moms* will guide you through the deep waters of tragedy and prepare you to uplift others who are in need of courage, love, laughter, and hope.

Fresh Elastic for STRETCHED OUT Moms

BARBARA JOHNSON

346.6

Fleming H. Revell
A Division of Baker Book House Co
Grand Rapids, Michigan 49516

© 2003 by Barbara Johnson

Published by Fleming H. Revell
a division of Baker Book House Company
P.O. Box 6287, Grand Rapids, MI 49516-6287
www.bakerbooks.com

Printed in the United States of America

Library of Congress Cataloging-in-Publication Data
Johnson, Barbara (Barbara E.)
    Fresh elastic for stretched out moms / by Barbara Johnson.
        p.   cm.
    Originally published: Old Tappan, N.J. : F.H. Revell, c1986.
    ISBN 0-8007-5859-5 (pbk.)
    1. Mothers—Religious life. 2. Mother and child. 3. Consolation. 4.
    Johnson, Barbara (Barbara E.) I. Title.
    BV4529.18 .J63 2003
    248.8′431—dc21   2002014649

Scripture quotations identified KJV are from the King James Version of the Bible.

Scripture quotations marked TLB are taken from *The Living Bible* © 1971. Used by permission of Tyndale House Publishers, Inc., Wheaton, IL 60189. All rights reserved.

Scripture quotations identified NIV are from the HOLY BIBLE, NEW INTERNATIONAL VERSION®. NIV®. Copyright © 1973, 1978, 1984 by International Bible Society. Used by permission of Zondervan Publishing House. All rights reserved.

Scripture quotation identified PHILLIPS is from LETTERS TO YOUNG CHURCHES by J. B. Phillips. Copyright © 1947, 1957 by Macmillan Publishing Co., Inc., renewed 1975 by J. B. Phillips. Used by permission.

"It's Friday . . . but Sunday's Coming" © 1983 by Marilyn Haverkate, Seed Sowers Calligraphy, 1220 165th Avenue, Monroe, WI 53566. Copies available.

"You Know You've Had a Rough Day When . . ."; "Dieting"; "You Know You Are a Mother When . . ." are taken from *Laughables*, Copyright ©

1984 by Harvest House Publishers, 1075 Arrowsmith, Eugene, OR 97402. Used by permission.

"Down With Pessimism," by Ron Wilson, is reprinted with permission of the author.

"Love Is the Greatest," by Carol M. Dettoni, copyright © 1981. Used by permission.

"Excuses, Excuses" is from *Looking at Language,* by Richard Lederer.

"Garment of Praise," copyright © 1978 by David Ingles Music, Tulsa, OK 74101. All rights reserved. Used by permission.

"The Vacant Sandbox," by Clarice Lancaster, appeared in *Sunshine* magazine and is used by permission of the author.

"God Washed the Earth," by Vickie Black, is used by permission.

Quotation from "The Love of God" by F. M Lehman, copyright 1917. Ren. 1945 by Nazarene Publishing House. Used by permission.

"Not-So-Famous Last Words" appears in the *Toronto Sun,* July 26,

1977, and is used by permission of Canada Wide/Toronto Sun.

Material from Gospel Light Publications, as published by *Family Life Today* magazine, Ventura, CA 93003 is used by permission.

Material by Charles Swindoll from the book *Growing Strong in the Seasons of Life* by Charles R. Swindoll, copyright © 1983 by Charles R. Swindoll. Published by Multnomah Press, Portland, OR 97266. Used by permission.

Quotation from "I Have Found Such Joy" in *Light of the Years* by Grace Noll Crowell, copyright 1936 by Harper & Row, Publishers, Inc. Renewed 1964 by Grace Noll Crowell. Reprinted by permission of Harper & Row, Publishers, Inc.

"To One in Sorrow" from *Songs of Hope* by Grace Noll Crowell, copyright 1938 by Harper & Row, Publishers, Inc. Renewed 1966 by Grace Noll Crowell. Reprinted by permission of Harper & Row, Publishers, Inc.

Diligent effort has been made to locate the author and copyright ownership of all quoted material included in this volume.

To our youngest son, Barney—

who has done the most to put fresh, new elastic into
my stretched out frazzled life

with

his loving way—
his wide smile—
his strong arm on my shoulder,
and by telling me I can make it

Contents

A Note from the Author . . .

It gives me great pleasure that my publisher is offering a new edition of *Fresh Elastic for Stretched Out Moms.* I wrote this book early in my writing career, and while all my books have their place in my heart, I have to confess that this one is my favorite. I liked it so much that I sometimes borrowed bits and pieces from it for my other books.

Why is it my favorite? I think because it's gentle. In *Fresh Elastic for Stretched Out Moms,* I don't require much of you, my dear reader. And even though it's organized along the twelve months of a calendar year, you can read it completely out of order if you want. Or even by opening it at random. I want you to relax and put no pressure on yourself. Do not feel you have to set aside a daily time to read. Do not take notes. Keep this book in the bathroom if you want. Be open. Let God minister to you in the gentlest of ways when you read it.

You'll find it is jam-packed with every inspirational story, ditty, quotation, and encouraging Scripture verse that I have saved over the years, the kinds of things we cut out of newspapers and put on the fridge. The kinds of things we tuck into cards to send to each other. The kinds of things we now e-mail to lists of friends who need encouraging. Again, let the words speak to you. Don't study them. Just open up and accept whatever healing can get through to you.

I have always maintained that since I've so thoroughly been in the darker trenches of life, I really do understand the pain you may be going through. This book was written as a result of many bouts with the emotional pain of living, mostly having to do with my sons and my husband.

Now I am living with the pain of an ailing physical body. I am presently undergoing chemotherapy for cancer that depletes my energy and sometimes even my zest for life. So how delighted I am to know that I can continue to share much of the inspiration I've gathered along the way in this book. It can continue to help you without my having to conjure up anything new!

What is in these pages is still fresh. Let it speak to you. And may God show his presence to you daily.

Introduction

Parents who have been devastated by a grown child in big trouble feel as if life isn't worth living anymore. They are so far down in the pit, no one can reach them. They are so stuck flat against the ceiling that no one can peel them off, even with a spatula. They are so far in left field that no one can even get a radar fix on them. They are so crushed, no one can pick them up. Their "elastic," which helps them to stretch through bad times, is all frayed and frazzled. If you have been hurt like that by one of your children, then you know what I mean. Maybe your child has a serious drug problem. Maybe your child has been critically injured in an automobile accident. Maybe your child has severed all relations with you, and you don't even know if he is alive or dead. Maybe your child has chosen a life of homosexuality, and you can't agree with it.

No matter what your child has done, you, and many parents like you, have experienced trauma and devastation in connection with a son or daughter. What you need is a caring person who has been there and can now reach out, bringing restoration and sanity to your hurting heart. You need some fresh elastic! I've been "on the ceiling" several times before—you might say I'm an expert on parent-devastation experiences.

Expert Credentials

In 1966 my husband, Bill, was critically injured in an automobile accident. I had been following his car up into the mountains when I found him sprawled in the middle of a high, winding, tortuous road, almost dead and severely brain-damaged. During the time when the doctors didn't think he would live, and then during his recovery, I had to learn to cope with parenting in a new and lonely way. I didn't know at the time that God was developing strength within me for the coming trials, those involving our children.

Then, in 1968, our son Steve was killed in Vietnam. I thought at first that no one could bear such pain and loss and still survive; but the grace and strength of God upheld me, and warm Christian friends provided the shoulders I needed for my tears, and the smiles I needed for recovery. In fact, God soon began using me to help other parents who had experienced the death of a child. God had "peeled" me off the ceiling once, and He was putting me to good use!

I was in the pits again in 1973. Our wonderful son Tim, who had just dedicated his life to Christ during the summer while he was vacationing in Alaska, was killed by a drunken driver in a horrible head-on collision on his way home. My immediate reaction was one of shock and anger: "It's unfair! Why would God take him now, just when he had begun sharing His love with others?" Then, slowly, I began to be aware through the circumstances that God had a plan to reach others through Tim's death—people Tim couldn't have reached if he had been alive.

Of course, I felt great grief and sorrow, but I also could see God's hand in the whole situation. As I stood in the mortuary, waiting to identify Tim's broken body, I was reliving an old, bad dream. This was the very same room, the same wallpaper, the same carpeting, the same everything as it had been when Steve was killed—except there was another box with another boy in it. How unbelievable that this could happen to us *twice*—just five years to the *day!*

I saw the shattered body and signed another paper stating that this was the right name to go with the crumpled body of our son. But God reminded me that this was not *Tim*. This was only his earthly shell. Tim was not there. And I began to see the glory in all this! It was as if I could look up and see Tim standing there, all bright and smiling at me, saying, "Don't cry, Mother. I am here with Jesus. I am finally Home! Don't feel bad." We tried to reflect that attitude at Tim's "Coronation Service." We didn't call it a funeral, because we were celebrating his triumphant homegoing. My sister and I wore green dresses—symbolizing life. We completed the uplifting service with the entire audience joining in the singing of "The Hallelujah Chorus." Tim's death launched us into one of the most exciting ministries I've ever known—helping other hurting parents to begin to live again!

Even though I was giving comfort to other parents, and rejoicing in the ministry God had built through tragedy, I didn't seriously think that anything else would happen (or could!). After all, I had paid my dues twice (three times, counting Bill's near death). It was time for me to "rest" on my recovery.

Broadsided Again

Imagine, then, how I felt the day before Father's Day in 1975 when I discovered, quite by accident, that our son Larry, age twenty, was a practicing homosexual! Remember, this was in the days before "gay liberation," and not only did I know homosexuality as evil, but I had all those fears of the unknown that were so prevalent then.

By accident, I discovered a drawer full of homosexual magazines in Larry's room, and he wasn't home for me to talk to. I had to drive immediately to the airport to pick up some relatives I hadn't seen since Tim's death two years before. I didn't know what to do, but I left a short note for Larry and headed for the airport. The drive was only a blur. I alternated between heaving sobs of stabbing pain and low moans like those of a dying person. Why couldn't we have just this one day together to make some good memories for us all, since it was the first time our family had been together since Tim's death two years ago? The pain in my chest was stabbing. My head was throbbing, and my throat felt as if it were stuffed with a shag rug. My mind whirled with thoughts of Larry—so irresistible as a little boy, so clever, so brilliant.

Immediately after we learned about his homosexuality, Larry left home abruptly, leaving no note, no phone number or address where we could get in touch with him. We had no idea whether we would ever see him again.

The next eleven months were horrible for me. I was stuck so flat against the ceiling that I thought I would never come down. All of that seems like a nightmare, more terrible than any actual nightmare, since I couldn't wake up from it. I kept a journal during that time. It was the only thing I could hang onto that I could do with any honesty. So often I just wanted to die, or to go to sleep and never wake up. I was really desperate, and even considered taking my own life. It wasn't until I turned the whole matter over to the Lord, that the burden rolled off my chest, my teeth quit itching, and the panic signs left. I could actually breathe and not feel pain. Then, slowly and gradually, God began to work in me. He used other Christians to minister to me, a little bit at a time. Recovery wasn't instantaneous, and it wasn't even very quick, but it came. Our youngest son, Barney, was an instrument used by God to help in my recovery, as was my dear husband, Bill. Inch by inch, I came unstuck from the ceiling. Moment by moment, day by day, the wrenching pain became a little bit less.

Spatula Ministries

As the healing came, so did a brand-new ministry. When I was in the depths of my depression, wishing I were dead, I looked in vain for some other parent with whom I could share this terrible secret and my horrible pain. My therapist, my husband, our youngest son, seventeen-year-old Barney, my sister, all of them helped in various ways. But what I really needed was somebody who could say, "I've been exactly where you are. I know how you feel because I experienced the same thing. And the good news is that you can survive!" Because I had no one to talk to who really knew how *I* felt, I kept it all inside.

That's what our *Spatula Ministries* is all about—we are parents who are hurting because of our children (whether the hurt is caused by death, rebellion, sin, sickness, or just indifference). We've been on the ceiling, stuck tight, and we are recovering (some are further along than others). We are the *spatulas* needed to peel parents off the ceiling and begin them on the road to recovery.

How I thank the Lord for each person I share this common burden with—whether that person is on the ceiling or doing the peeling! On days when it seems all this work is so in vain, and we get some calls which are threatening, or people are so critical (thinking that when we show love to our wayward children, we are condoning their actions), those are the days when I wonder what is so great about hanging in there. For what? And then I remember the final reward: standing before the Lord and knowing I have fought a good fight, have kept the faith, and have finished the course.

Working for the Lord

It's great! The pay isn't much, but the retirement plan is just out of this world! And always when discouragement strikes, I think about each parent out there who is hurting, just as I was hurting, and who needs to know that it is possible to survive, and even to be victorious over something that seems so terrible. Our ministry is, as Dr. James Dobson says, ". . . to prop people up when they are unable to stand alone." We are the propper-uppers, but it works both ways. I also receive a tremendous amount of propping up from those I have helped. They are there to prop me up when the waves of despair and discouragement come, when friends tell me to go back into the flow of life, and forget what God called me for.

The Lord gave us this ministry, and until they put a lily in my hand, and close the casket over me, I know we have to be here to prop others up who are sinking. We can be a warm hand in the dark, black pit—a refresher to those with no refreshment. How blessed it is to be a fresher-upper!

God Uses the Available

God can use anyone to help those who are hurting. He'll even draft people if He needs to! Let me give you an example. Spatula Ministries is not listed in the telephone book and the only way anyone can get our number is through reading my first book, or from the Billy Graham Evangelistic Association, or Dr. Dobson's "Focus on the Family," or from the Crystal Cathedral, where we have our meetings. Now we have a phone book listing under "Barbara Spatula Johnson." Before that many people asked directory assistance for *Barbara Johnson* in La Habra, and instead of me, they got this darling little old lady who has been getting lots and lots of calls since the publication of my book *Where Does a Mother Go to Resign?* came out. It was only recently that she finally learned why her phone was so busy.

This is what happened. I got a call from an elderly woman, telling me her name was Barbara Johnson. She said that for the past couple of years she had had people calling her at all hours of the day and night, and they were crying. They would pour out such a story of woe, and it was always interesting, she said, but she had no idea why they were calling *her*. Finally, one day she was in the grocery store and saw my first book on a rack. She immediately bought it and read it straight through. Then she realized why she was getting so many calls. People had mentioned *spatula* but she had no information on it, and they were always crying, so that she listened attentively and tried to say something helpful, but she had no idea how she had become such a sought-after person.

The "other" Mrs. Johnson said it was the most excitement she had experienced in years. Furthermore, she said that when folks call her in the middle of the night or early in the morning, she tells them "not to wake that dear lady at this hour, but call back when California folks get up!"

That's what I mean when I say that God uses those who are available—not those who think they know everything and can handle everything! If you are stuck on the ceiling, look around for those who are *available* to help, and thank God that you *will* recover—even if it takes the rest of your life.

Happy New Year

You can begin your recovery *today*. You don't have to wait another minute. This can be "New Year's Day" for your Year of Recovery. God has given us measurements of time (like seasons) to help us get some perspective on our lives. If you can't measure time, you can't *handle* time. Don't think of this time on the ceiling as an eternity—it's not. It just seems like it! Every minute you spend stuck

18

to the ceiling over your wayward child is just a minute. *It's not a life sentence.*

I won't pretend that recovery is easy or quick. It is neither. It's hard work and commitment, but it does happen. God is waiting to help you begin your first day of recovery. Take Him up on His offer, and start your new Year of Recovery today.

Help Is on the Way!

This book is designed to help you. We've used the symbolic theme of months to "walk" with you through your pain and into happiness. I *know* what you have to go through to survive—I've done it myself. Take my hand, as one who's been there, and take Jesus' hand, as the only One who can pull you through, and together we can win!

The selections I have made for this book will help you to cope through a down time. It will bring you out of the pits. It won't be a fast trip, but you need to grow through it. There may even be a time when you think you have "matured" through August, and then some new devastation will send you back to March. *But* you will eventually have victory. I don't want you to go under, I don't want to drown you with platitudes that don't give permanent growth. I want to share with you what worked for me, and what's working for others in the same boat.

Your Year of Recovery

Begin with January, *even if you're reading this in August.* When we are devastated by our kids, it seems like a bleak, cold, dead January day anyway! January is our month of *newness,* for *putting aside the past.* January will give you *encouragement* to believe you can drop the past and start over. Now you can start "setting" your new elastic.

In February, we concentrate on showing *unconditional love and forgiveness,* the foundation for moving on through the recovery process. We need to move along slowly and gently, growing and progressing. That which grows slowly *endures.* I don't want you to be on some big emotional high, thinking you have it made, and then be totally devastated all over again when some other problem comes along, washing you back to sea, drowning again in your sorrow. You don't have to go back again!

March teaches us *how to deal with reality*—as ugly as it sometimes is. When you know you can start over again, and when you are secure in the unconditional love of the Lord, then you can begin to come to grips with the heavy times in life. (Heavy-duty elastic may be required here.)

April is our *fun month.* We need a break from reality sometimes, don't you think? April is for "fools." It is lightness. It is the shine and luster needed after the serious business of March.

May is our *hope* chapter. You will have learned about being in the pits, and you will have begun your climb out of the pits. You'll have learned how to laugh at yourself and life. May will give you *encouragement.* You eventually will feel better. May is the light at the end of the tunnel, and that light isn't from another train coming along! May is a big knot at the end of the rope, reminding you that you can hang in there—and even climb up. Believe that you will get through your sorrow, and lift up your drooping hands and sad hearts. Pull that elastic a little tighter.

In June we decorate our desert. We learn *how we can take positive steps toward changing our lives and the world around us.* We might be stuck in the desert, but we can make that desert look pretty good with the decorations we choose!

After we prepare our deserts in June, then July helps us to *acknowledge that while life isn't always the way we want it, no tragedy lasts forever.* Recovery and survival are in reach. We can walk together, patiently enduring the sorrow and depression, as we grow up from the valley, onto the mountaintop. Sorrow may flood you repeatedly, but each time you will survive, stronger and happier than before. You will bounce back quicker and not stay down so long. Your new elastic has more resiliency.

When a parent is consumed with grief, he or she needs some relief. Especially for those of us with grown children, age and weight loom threateningly close. August is our month to *poke fun at age and weight.* When we are in the pits, our mirror shows the strain and pain we have come through. We feel so alone in this battle. For those of us who are living between estrogen and death, our attitude can make all the difference in the world. We can feel less alone—and we can learn to laugh at what we felt was impossible to accept before.

September is a *nostalgic month* for us parents who no longer have kids to bundle off to school. Memories seem to flood us of other years, when kids were small and starting school. We think about mistakes we have made in our children's lives. Aches flood our memories of situations in the past which need healing. So *September is our month for learning about constructive memories,* making new ones

21

for the future, enjoying memories which may not have been of perfect times, but in which we can find a reason to rejoice. Today's experiences are tomorrow's memories. September will inject some healing into places where there are raw edges in your emotional memories.

October is the month when fall really takes hold. *It reminds us that the battle isn't over yet.* We are trying to grow, but we are sometimes held back by new problems and our still immature attempts to deal with them. October is *reality—learning to accept what we have.* Nothing is perfect, nothing will be exactly right, but we can enjoy and *appreciate* what we have, not what we wish we had. We need to learn to accept what God has for us.

In November, we can *learn to let go*—to be thankful for what God has done, to do our best, and then to let go: of the pain, the suffering, the worry, our children. When we have done our best, we have to let our children go and leave them in God's hands.

December is *about maturing; how problems have brought us to a point where we can handle them.* We do not sink and drown, because we are *survivors.* We have come through the fire and been tried. We have our credentials. We are *winners!*

We have learned the secrets of survival, and learned how to help others through the deep waters of tragedy. We have been given things to overcome and we have become overcomers! This is a chapter of *victory.*

We have learned how joy is infused. That is the secret of this book. After the learning period you will be able to see how the real joy of the Lord has been wallpapered to your heart, and it will not peel off! Deep, lasting joy will be with you in every situation in life. You will make it; you will have hope, courage, maturity, and joy. *Real* joy is having God living in the marrow of your bones.

Let's Go!

My prayer is that these messages will take you through your Year of Recovery. Together we will walk through your depression. We can't shove, push, or dump heaps of advice on you. Advice is like snow—the softer it falls, the deeper it sinks! Begin your new year today, and join the survivors whose old, worn-out, stretched elastic has been replaced slowly and surely by fresh, resilient, *new* elastic!

January

The Land of Beginning Again

I wish that there were some wonderful place
    Called the Land of Beginning Again,
Where all our mistakes and all our heartaches
    And all of our selfish grief
Could be dropped like a shabby, old coat at the door,
    And never be put on again.

I wish we could come on it all unaware,
    Like the hunter who finds a lost trail;
And I wish that the one whom our blindness has done
    The greatest injustice of all
Could be at the gates like an old friend that waits
    For the comrade he's gladdest to hail.

We would find all the things we intended to do
    But forgot, and remembered too late,
Little praises unspoken, little promises broken,
    And all of the thousand and one
Little duties neglected that might have perfected
    The day for one less fortunate.

It wouldn't be possible not to be kind
In the Land of Beginning Again;
And the ones we misjudged and the ones whom we
    grudged
Their moments of victory here
Would find in the grasp of our loving handclasp
More than penitent lips could explain.

For what had been hardest we'd know had been best,
    And what had seemed lost would be gain;
For there isn't a sting that will not take wing
    When we've faced it and laughed it away;
And I think that the laughter is most what we're after
    In the Land of Beginning Again.

So I wish that there were some wonderful place
    Called the Land of Beginning Again,
Where all our mistakes and all our heartaches
    And all of our poor selfish grief
Could be dropped like a shabby, old coat at the door,
    And never be put on again.

LOUISA FLETCHER

What God's Fresh Elastic Can Do

January is a fresh new month, the "land of beginning again." God's fresh elastic can pull you together once more. You *can* make a brand-new start in your life. No matter what has happened in the past, that is over. No matter how much you wish the past had been different, especially concerning your wayward child, you cannot change what has already happened. Don't mourn over what is done; rejoice that there is still a future! Yesterday is a canceled check, tomorrow is a promissory note, but today is cash! Use it wisely. Today you can have a new refreshing love, a return to Christian fellowship, a new friendship, a new dream. Yes, you can have a fresh, new start in January. Tear off that old calendar month, and enjoy that fresh new page with no blot or scars on it.

God is present and ready to help you right where you are. Reach out in a simple prayer to Jesus and feel Him now take your hand. With His hand and power at work in your life, you, too, can have your tears turned into joy, your night into day, your pain into gain, your failures into successes, your scars into stars, and your tragedy into triumph. Put the canceled checks behind you and the future in God's hands. Enjoy the cash at hand, and your new start today!

Life would be unbearable for many of us parents if it were not for the opportunity of a fresh, new beginning. Just imagine, God even designed nature to give us 365 brand-new days every year. That is 365 new starts, and twelve months of fresh starts thrown in as a bonus! God made every day to be a new day!

Because Jesus lives for you, a new day is dawning. He is the One who makes all things new. Reach out in a simple prayer to Him. If you fail in one place, that doesn't make you a failure. Sure, we all fall, but it's how long you stay down that counts. Get up, begin again, and you will know the joy of a fresh start with Jesus.

The mail to our ministry from hurting parents is just bursting with exciting letters and stories of changes in relationships; some tell of terrible pain and suffering, but many of transition and progress in the journey of understanding others. One special parent, for example, who is "beginning again" sent me a wonderful little plaque which reads:

> ## Joy is not the absence of suffering, but the presence of God.

We all go through pain and sorrow, but the presence of God, like a warm comforting blanket, can shield us and protect us, and allow the deep inner joy to surface, even in the most devastating circumstances. I know, because I have been there.

I have used this poem to help myself and other parents to let go of the past, with all of its mistakes and heartaches, and to hang on to God's promises for today. Read these words, and promise God to "begin today" to form a new outlook on your problems and pain.

BEGIN TODAY

Dream not too much of what you'll do tomorrow,
    How well you'll work another year;
Tomorrow's chance you do not need to borrow—
    Today is here.
Boast not too much of mountains you will master
    The while you linger in the vale below,
To dream is well, but plodding brings us faster
    To where we go.
Talk not too much about some new endeavor
    You mean to make a little later on.
Who idles now will idle on forever
    'Til life is gone.
Swear not some day to break some habit's fetter,
    When this old year is dead and passed away;
If you have need of living wiser, better,
    Begin today.

AUTHOR UNKNOWN

New Year's Resolutions

Most people think of the month of January as the month for New Year's resolutions. I don't usually like the idea of New Year's resolutions. I hate to wait a whole year to try to mend a mistake, and find that when I put off changes, I don't change at all. However, the New Year's resolutions below have helped me tremendously, and I hope they will help you, too. (And you don't have to make them only on New Year's—they bring healing and spiritual health all year long.)

❀ I will, like Paul, forget those things which are behind and press forward.

❀ I will, like David, lift up mine eyes unto the hills from whence comes help.

❀ I will, like Abraham, trust implicitly in my God.

❀ I will, like Enoch, walk in daily fellowship with my Heavenly Father.

❀ I will, like Jehoshaphat, prepare my heart to seek God.

❀ I will, like Moses, choose rather to suffer than enjoy the pleasures of sin.

❀ I will, like Daniel, commune with my God at all times.

❀ I will, like Job, be patient under all circumstances.

❀ I will, like Gideon, stand firm even though my friends be few.

❀ I will, like Aaron, uphold the hands of my spiritual leader.

❀ I will, like Isaiah, consecrate myself to God's work.

❀ I will, like Andrew, strive to lead my brother to a closer walk with Christ.

❀ I will, like John, lean upon the bosom of the Master.

- **I will, like Stephen, manifest a forgiving spirit toward all who hurt me.**
- **I will, like the Heavenly Host, proclaim the message of peace and good will.**

I know this list is a tall order for change, and you may feel that only a spiritual giant could do all of those things. But even spiritual giants started out with just one step. If you feel like a spiritual pygmy, or a spiritual munchkin, don't despair. If you can follow through on just one of these resolutions, you will be making some real progress, right?

Celebrate *Your* Day!

I have always looked forward to celebrating the first day of each new month. How I LOVE to tear off the calendar page and see a fresh new month! I have lots of ways to celebrate. I wash my hair, take a bath, change the sheets, and really *make* it a holiday to pamper myself. The first day of each new month is sort of a Celebrate Me day!

I celebrate me!
I am worth everything.
I am unique.
In the whole world there is only one me.
There is only one person with my talents, my experiences, and my gifts.
No one can take my place.
God created only one me, precious in His sight.
It doesn't matter my age, color, or whether I was loved as a child or not. Let all that go. That belongs to the past. I belong to the *Now!* It doesn't matter where I have been, or mistakes I've made or hurts I have had.

I am forgiven. I am accepted. I'm okay. I am loved in
spite of everything. **CELEBRATE ME!** Begin now.
I am temporarily here today and gone tomorrow.

But *today,* today can be a fresh day, a new beginning. This
earth suit will be gone one day, traded in for a robe of white—
until then I have *today* to enjoy because I deserve to *celebrate* **me!**

Yes, you *can* make the first day of each month a special day for yourself . . . pamper yourself on this day . . .
open only mail which is good (no bills). Do something
fun for yourself that *you* really enjoy. Take off that mask
of adulthood and be a child again. You can tap into a
boundless fountain of youth within yourself, if you spend
these bonus days letting that child come out. Take this
day to throw off your rigidity, and recapture that childlike spontaneity, so you can be at peace with yourself. You
deserve these bonus days! Enjoy yourself!

How Would You Like to Live Your Life Over?

We can't really live our whole lives over again, but we
can make progress from where we are right now to where
God wants us to be. The only time it's too late to change
our lives is when we reach heaven—God's eternal today.
However, I know all of us, especially hurting parents, sometimes wish we could live our whole lives over again, not
making the many mistakes which our hindsight points out
to us. Consider what Brother Jeremiah says on this subject:

If I Had My Life to Live Over
If I had my life to live over again, I'd try to make more mistakes next time. I would relax. I would limber up. I would

be sillier than I have been this trip. I know of a very few things I would take seriously. I would take more trips. I would climb more mountains, swim more rivers and watch more sunsets. I would do more walking and looking. I would eat more ice cream and fewer beans. I would have more actual troubles and fewer imaginary ones. You see, I am one of those people who lives prophylactically and sensibly and sanely hour after hour, day after day. Oh, I've had my moments; and if I had it to do over again, I'd have more of them. In fact, I'd try to have nothing else. Just moments, one after another, instead of living so many years ahead each day. I have been one of those people who never go anywhere without a thermometer, a hot water bottle, a gargle, a rain-coat, aspirin and a parachute. If I had it to do over again, I would go places, do things and travel lighter than I have.

If I had my life to live over, I would ride on more merry-go-rounds—pick more daisies.

BROTHER JEREMIAH

BEGIN AGAIN

Every day is a fresh beginning,
    Every morn is the world made new.
You who are weary of sorrow and sinning,
    Here is a beautiful hope for you,—
    A hope for me and a hope for you.
Every day is a fresh beginning;
    Listen, my soul, to the glad refrain,
And, in spite of old sorrow and older sinning,
    And puzzles forecasted and possible pain,
    Take heart with the day, and begin again.

SUSAN COOLIDGE

Golden Minutes

Along with the theme of Beginning Again is this little poem about the minutes of life—so small they're easily lost, but so important that they can shape the future. Take this message to heart, and don't waste your minutes, the "change" of today's "cash."

MINUTES OF GOLD

Two or three minutes—two or three hours,
What do they mean in this life of ours?
   But minutes of gold and hours sublime,
   If only we'll use them once in a while
   To make someone happy—make someone smile.
A minute may dry a little lad's tears,
An hour sweep aside the trouble of years.
   Minutes of my time may bring to an end
Hopelessness somewhere, and bring me a friend.

AUTHOR UNKNOWN

It's Not Over Till It's Over

I know how hard it is for hurting parents to let go of the past, live in today, and have hope for tomorrow. Many times I am asked for words of comfort to parents whose kids are on a "detour" from God's best for them, or kids into rebellion. We *don't give the final score on a life until the game is over.* In most of our kids' lives, it isn't even *halftime* yet. God doesn't promise us that we'll be leading at the half, but He did promise we would win the game!

If you are grieving over a lost child right now, as are most of the parents who write me, these words are for you to put up in a prominent place, to remember them as daily exhortations: *God didn't promise we'd be leading at the half, but only that we would win the game!* You can recover and gain confidence in your children by remembering that loving your child is a long-term investment, not a short-term loan. Loving that child unconditionally, even when you know he is in sin, doing wrong, and acting hatefully toward the family that tries to show him love, is what will finally pay off for you. Love is worth the time it takes to grow, and growing a child is not a quick process. Remember that the victory is ours at the *end* of all this.

Waiting on God is resting instead of worrying. You can fake waiting. Ever tried to fake it? We all have. We can fret down inside and put that plastic smile on that says we're really at peace when we're not—we're retching inside; we're panic-stricken.

Change of Perspective

It's amazing how one's attitude about something can change with a different perspective. I heard this account about a college girl which is a good example of that. The young college freshman had just finished semester finals and wrote her parents this letter:

> Dear Mom and Dad,
> Just thought I'd drop you a note to clue you in on my plans. I've fallen in love with a guy called Jim. He quit high school after grade 11 to get married. About a year ago he got a divorce. We've been going steady for two months, and we plan to get married in the fall. Until then, I've decided to move into his apartment. (I think I might be pregnant.) At any rate, I dropped out of school last week, although I'd like to finish college sometime in the future.

On the next page she continued her letter:

Mom and Dad, I just want you to know that everything I've written so far in this letter is false. None of it is true. But Mom and Dad, it is true that I got a C– in French and I flunked math. And it's true that I'm going to need a lot more money for my tuition payments.

What this young woman did was to give her mom and dad some perspective. She set them up to accept anything.

That's what failure is all about. If you compare it with the opinion of man, you'll go right down the tubes, and you'll stay down there for months. If you compare it with the Lord's "lovingkindness," that goes from everlasting to everlasting, you can't stay down. God uses even our failures to make better people of us. Jesus saw men, not as they were, but as they were to become, filled with His Spirit and dedicated to His work. There's nothing wrong with failure. There's plenty wrong with giving up. If you are splattered against the ceiling as a result of failures in your life or the lives of your children, don't just give up and stay there. Get help so you can get peeled off the ceiling and begin recovery. *God will not leave you on the ceiling!* He will bring healing, patience, and comfort when you don't think you can sur-

A New Day

This is the beginning of a new day. God has given me this day to use as I will. I can waste it—or use it for good, but what I do today is important, because I am exchanging a day of my life for it! When tomorrow comes, this day will be gone forever, leaving in its place something that I have traded for it. I want it to be gain, and not loss; good, and not evil; success, and not failure; in order that I shall not regret the price that I have paid for it.

vive another day. Don't grieve over the past; rejoice that God has already planned the future!

Say Good-Bye to the Past

I can't emphasize enough that for true recovery to begin, you must be able to let go of the past. Throw out your old calendar, even if it's only May when you read this. No matter what the time of year, today can begin a New Year for you! Get yourself a sunny new calendar, full of pages still blank, still waiting to be filled in with exciting experiences from God's plan.

Your New Year is going to be a Year of Recovery, a year of relearning some of the "lessons of life" that you didn't quite get the first time around. Most of us are long past the time of going to school, studying, and taking tests. Most of us are even past preparing our children for school and tests. But no matter what our ages, we are never too old to learn, and these lessons are worth every bit of study and practice you can give them.

Nine Lessons for the New Year

1. Learn to laugh. A good laugh is better than medicine.
2. Learn to tell a story. A well-told story is as welcome as a sunbeam in a sickroom.
3. Learn the art of saying kind and encouraging things.
4. Learn to avoid all ill-natured remarks and everything likely to create friction.
5. Learn to keep your troubles to yourself. The world is too busy to care for your ills and sorrows.

6. Learn to stop grumbling. If you cannot see any good in the world, keep the bad to yourself.

7. Learn to hide your aches and pains under a pleasant smile. No one cares whether you have a headache or rheumatism.

8. Learn to greet your friends with a smile. They carry too many frowns in their own hearts to be bothered with any of yours.

9. Through the wetness of your tears, your own sorrow will begin to glisten. You can go from the pits, where it is black, to beige, and then to rainbows, which come from tears in our lives. Your constant habit of being a joy collector will be your therapy. Collect all the things which are lifters, not sinkers. You need encouragement and lightness. Start looking for it!

And Remember!

How we look at life can determine where we will find joy in our exercise of beginning again. This is what I wish for you in your New Year of Recovery: that you will find joy in sorrow, let go of the past, and embrace the future God has planned for you.

Yes, your New Year is just beginning. Don't worry about the past, and don't borrow trouble from the future. Be thankful that God has given you today, and work on using today's cash wisely. Life is not over just because you have experienced a devastating blow concerning your wayward child. Begin again today, and trust God's forgiveness to take care of yesterday, and His grace to take care of tomorrow.

February

A Soft Pillow for a Tired Heart

"And we know that all things work together for good to them that love God . . ." (Rom. 8:28 KJV). This is Scripture's soft pillow for a tired heart!

Now that you have started your walk in "the land of beginning again," your first step takes you to that which we all need: *Love.*

February is the month for love. My gift to you hurting parents this month is the reminder that the love of God never fails. Even when our parental love, like our old elastic, seems all spent and wasted, even when our best intentions and prayers seem to have produced children who reject us *and* the Lord, God's love never fails.

I often share this about the love of God: We pray, "Lord, I have sinned and fallen away from You. I am no longer worthy to be called Your child," and God replies: "My child, I know, but My son is eternally worthy to be called your Savior."

That's the love of God. Read the first five or six verses of Romans chapter five. This tells us that even when we were sinners, God loved us so much that He sent His Son to die for us. God's love never fails, and it can heal our hurting parents' hearts as well as mend our children's rebellious hearts. I am absolutely convinced that life does not happen by chance. God has a *plan;* God's plan is full of His love for us; and God's plan will succeed! When we are in the midst of pain it is hard to believe that, but I know it's true, and I've seen it work! This poem gives comfort and encouragement to believe that God's love will work out His plan in His time.

THINGS DON'T JUST HAPPEN

Things don't just happen to us who love God,
  They're planned by His own dear hand,
Then molded and shaped, and timed by His clock,
  Things don't just happen—they're planned.

We don't just guess on the issues of life;
  We Christians just rest in our Lord,
We are directed by His sovereign will,
  In the light of His holy Word.

We who love Jesus are walking by faith,
  Not seeing one step that's ahead,
Not doubting one moment what our lot might be,
  But looking to Jesus, instead.

We praise our dear Saviour for loving us so,
  For planning each care of our life;
Then giving us faith to trust Him for all
  The blessings as well as the strife.

Things don't just happen to us who love God,
  To us that have taken our stand;

No matter the lot, the course, or the price,
Things don't just happen, they're planned.

Esther L. Fields

Unconditional Love

With Valentine's Day being my very own special day (which I love more than any other), I wanted to share this story about unconditional love, the kind of love we need for our wayward children, even when they are hurting us:

A little boy who had moved into a new neighborhood was quiet and shy. His name was Brad. He came home one day and told his mom he knew Valentine's Day was coming, and he wanted to make a valentine for everyone in his class. His mother's heart sank, and she wished he wouldn't do that. Every afternoon she had watched all the kids coming home from school, laughing and hanging onto each other, books under their arms. All except for Brad. He walked along behind them, alone.

But Brad was determined, and so she went along with his idea, buying him glue, paper, and crayons. For three weeks, Brad painstakingly made thirty-five paper valentines. When the day came to deliver the valentines, he was so excited! This was his day! He stacked those valentines under his arm and ran out the door to school. His mother thought, *This will be a tough day for Brad. I'm going to bake some cookies and give him some milk, when he comes in from school. That will ease the pain. He probably won't get many valentines.*

That afternoon she had the warm cookies and milk on the table. She went to the window and watched anxiously for the children. Sure enough, there came a big gang of children, all laughing, valentines under their arms. They had really done well. And then there was Brad, trudging along

The Shield of Love

When I felt
That touch of spring
Yesterday
I washed my car
and waxed it.
When it rained
This morning
The droplets
On the hood
Stood upright
In tiny bubbles
Unable to penetrate
That coat of wax.

When I prayed to God
Last night
He must have washed my
  soul,
Bathed it in His love
Because
Today
When troubles came
They only
Stood outside
Unable to penetrate
That shield of love.

behind them, alone again. He walked faster than usual and she thought, *Bless his heart; he is ready to burst into tears. His arms are empty!*

He came in the house and she scooped him into her arms, saying, "Darling, Mommy has some warm cookies and milk for you!" But his face was aglow, a smile lit his eyes. "I didn't forget a single one, Mom, not a single one!" His pride and joy shone through every word.

Don't forget to love your child unconditionally! He or she may pierce your heart with actions which seem to you to be designed especially to hurt you. But your job is not to judge, not to condemn, not to get revenge. Your job as a Christian and a parent is to *love* that child in the midst of everything! If you clutch your love close to you, unwilling to share it unless you are absolutely safe, then your love will disappear all by itself and you will be left with nothing at all. Life's greatest joy is to give your love away. As you allow God's love to flow through you and you give that love out, God will use you to touch another person who needs to feel the warmth of that love.

Love Isn't Love Until You Give It Away

It would be great if we could all be spendthrifts and just buy anything in sight. But we *can* be spendthrifts in love! Love is the one treasure that is multiplied by division. It is the one gift that grows bigger the more you take from it. It is the one business in which it pays to be an absolute spendthrift. Give it away! Throw it away! Splash it over! Empty your pockets! Shake the basket, turn the glass upside down, and tomorrow you will have more than ever!

"Love wasn't put in your heart to stay, for love isn't love until you give it away." How much more is God's love given to us in abundance. The words to the song "The Love of God" were found scrawled on the wall of a mental hospital, but they contain such truth:

> Could we with ink the ocean fill,
> and were the skies of parchment made,
> Were every stalk on earth a quill,
> and every man a scribe by trade;
> To write the love of God above,
> would drain the ocean dry;
> Nor could the scroll contain the whole
> though stretched from sky to sky.

When you have "down" days (and we all do) and you feel that the black pit has you again, just dwell on God's love. How rich and full it is! Let His love keep you and give you rest. Think of Romans 8:28: "in all things God works for the good of those who love him" (NIV). And lay your tired heart down on that soft pillowy verse. Just rest in God's love, which is a shield around your hurting heart.

A Special Valentine

I received a very special Valentine's Day gift from a very special mother. It was two scented padded clothes hangers with some padded sachets with the word LOVE printed all over the satin covering. What is so special about it is that it was from the very first mother I ever counseled who had a homosexual son. At that time she lived near us and was desperate and sick from learning the truth. Now God has brought her and her family to glorious reward for all of her suffering and pain. The card with the gift had this note:

> Dear Barb:
> During the past few years our "closet" doors were opened and we didn't like what we saw, but now when you open your closet, this gift will remind you of my LOVE for you and how God turns ashes into beauty. I'm remembering how God sent me to you to help me grow, and I love Him and you so very much.

See how the fragrance from God works? We cannot pour love on others without spilling it on ourselves. So now, when I open my closet, I get a lovely scent from the hangers and the sachets. I see the word LOVE coming at me, and it reminds me of being ambushed with love. That is the secret of blessing in our lives, being able to ambush others with love and have God return it to us in a million ways.

Don't be afraid to share your love. Don't be afraid to give your love to a wayward child. Nothing will happen to you and your love that God isn't ultimately in charge of. He will give you the strength to risk your love, and the glue if your heart breaks and needs mending.

THE HEART

This heart of mine is such a fragile thing.
Like fine porcelain. I could set it on a shelf,
but I tend to put it rather in the midst of life.
Thus it has been broken a million times.
Perhaps the glue with which God mends it
is stronger than the stuff of which it is made.
Knowing that His blood was shed to make me whole,
encourages me to pick up the pieces, go on, and love
    again.
My heart is not a very pretty thing,
with all these cracks and mars and flaws.
But I feel. And it is certainly much more loving
Than a heart that is never touched at all.

AUTHOR UNKNOWN

Some folks feel sad during holiday times. Valentine's Day can be pretty cheerless when our hearts are hurting. Maybe you used to have fun with your children on Valentine's Day, with kids' parties and valentines to be signed for school. Some of us have kids that are gone. Other parents have such bad relationships with their children that they sometimes feel they would like to send a Valentine arrow to their child with a poisoned dart on it (just kidding)! But let's concentrate on making February a love month. Let's learn to love life and it will love us back.

What you give is what you get. Life is like a boomerang—
if you throw it out it will come back to you.

What Is This Thing Called Love?

Instead of seeing one big problem after another, let's
look for possibilities for lifting others, and opportunities
to enrich those around us. *Love* is an *action* word. You
have to show love.

So many people are lonely today. Every time you give
someone else a lift, you get a lift. Compassion is one healing, uplifting gift that God gives to each of us to use. Warm
compassion can break the chains that bind us and transform a cold, indifferent world into a warm, loving one.

Who does God use? He uses people like *you* and *me*.
Don't let past failures hinder you. Failure is a tough teacher,
but a good one. Let God's love flow through you to help
those who are hurting, needing the love you can release to
them. I tacked these words about love up in my kitchen,
where I could see them as I fixed meals and washed dishes.
They helped me to remember the perspective in which I
should put my love.

Love is . . .

Slow to suspect . . . quick to trust.

Slow to condemn . . . quick to justify.

Slow to offend . . . quick to defend.

Slow to reprimand . . . quick to forbear.

Slow to belittle . . . quick to appreciate.

Slow to demand . . . quick to give.

Slow to provoke . . . quick to conciliate.
Slow to hinder . . . quick to help.
Slow to resent . . . quick to forgive.

After I thought I had really learned these truths, I took them down from my cupboard door and replaced them with other words of wisdom, which I still get a charge out of each time I read.

God's love is expressed through other people to us. You don't have to be a perfect saint to be able to share love with someone else. You don't even have to be especially mature as a Christian to share God's love. You just have to be willing and be open. God's love is like a fragrant balm that does double duty. When you spread God's love balm on someone else, it not only heals that person but brings healing to you as well.

A Special Phone Call

The other day I was awakened by a phone call, which is not too unusual. But this call was different. Instead of coming from a desperate crying mother, it was from a very close friend, Maida. Her voice was squeaky, toneless, lacking in musical ability, but it

Love's ABC's

You'll have your hands full and your heart filled trying to live out Love's ABC's.

Love **A**ccepts, **B**ehaves, **C**heers, **D**efends, **E**nriches, **F**orgives, **G**rows, and **H**elps.

Love **I**ncludes, **J**oins, **K**neels, **L**istens, **M**otivates, **N**otices, **O**verlooks, and **P**rovides.

Love **Q**uiets, **R**espects, **S**urprises, **T**ries, **U**nderstands, **V**olunteers, **W**arms, e**X**pects, and **Y**ields.

Love in action breaks the code that adds **Z**ip to your life!

was singing one of my very favorite songs to me: "You are loved, you are loved, I have risked loving you, For the one who knows me best, loves you most." (Based on "I Am Loved" by William J. and Gloria Gaither, © copyright 1978 by William J. Gaither. All rights reserved. Used by permission.) What a sure way to start the day!

And Maida was not without problems herself that morning. She had just lost her son, who was murdered by gangsters, and she was on the way to Florida to buy a marker for his grave. And yet, at the busy airport, she took the time to call me and make my day sparkle! That is really what this kind of ministry is all about: hurting people reaching out to others who are hurting, to help bind up the wounds, to ask God to bring healing, and to share the love of God, "which passes all understanding." The following piece is perfect for hurting mothers who, like us, need to be reminded that a mother's love is unconditional—it comes in spite of what our children do.

LOVE IS THE GREATEST
(A PERSONAL RESPONSE TO I CORINTHIANS 13)

Love is patient. Boots, mittens, scarves, hats, sneakers, socks, schoolbooks, records, dolls, blocks, cars, glasses, dishes . . . from the front door through the whole house I find a messy path to follow! *How many times do I have to tell them to pick things up?*
Love is kind. "Mom, could you take me and six of my friends to the game?" *I will, but I really had other plans.*
Love does not envy. "Christine's house is so much bigger and nicer than ours." *I know. Every time I drive by that brown house, I wish I could live there.*

Love is not rude. "Are you ready to leave yet? I thought you said it would only be a minute." *I'm coming! Can you ever be more patient?*

Love is not self-seeking. "Could you bake a dozen cookies and help sell them at your daughter's grade-school Country Store next week?" *They always have something for me to do. But I had better be nice to her and do it. I may need her friendship sometime.*

Love is not easily angered. "I can't believe you'd do anything that stupid! Don't you ever think first!" *If you raise your voice at me again, I'm going to lose control.*

Love keeps no records of wrongs. "Honey, I really am sorry I forgot your birthday. Things at work and here at home kept me so busy, the date crept up on me." *I won't forget this! Ten years from now, I'll still remember!*

Love does not delight in evil, but rejoices in truth. "Did you hear about Jane's husband? He may be having problems at work." *Not only that. He's never home.*

Many are the ways to show love. A positive reinforcement stated, a note written, a diaper changed, a meal cooked, a soft word spoken, a tub of dirty clothes washed, a pat of reassurance given, a kiss of unrestrained passion shared, a car repaired, a flower sent, a loving spirit lived!

Love never fails. My love for my husband and children may falter and waver. Christ's love is unfailing.

Love always: *protects*—I want to take the hurt for my child. Instead, I will protect and love him.

> *trusts*—I trust, even when my husband travels a lot and faces life's temptations.
>
> *hopes*—We still share our dreams for life together.
>
> *perseveres*—Another obstacle in our lives? With God's sustaining power, we'll "tough it out" together!

Now these three remain: faith, hope, and love. *Love is the greatest.*

AUTHOR UNKNOWN

Give Him All the Pieces

God will mend a broken heart, but He must have *all* the pieces. When you are hurting, really in despair over your child who has left you and all the values you tried so hard to nurture in him, it is easy to show that your heart is broken. It lies in pieces all over your life, mute testimony to the depths of your love for your child and the depths of your hurt over his problems. But God can heal your heart. God can rescue you from despair and give you something to rejoice about again. It won't happen overnight: there is some necessary mourning and recovery you have to go through first, but *it will happen*. All you have to do is be willing to give every piece of your broken heart to God. Don't save a little piece in case you want to feel sorry for yourself. Don't save a little piece to use in your "martyred mother" role, where you suffer "righteously" because of your child's cruelty. Don't save a little piece to make yourself feel guilty over whatever blame you have for your child's problems. And be sure not to save a little piece that you can use to make your child feel guilty for the way he or she is hurting Mother.

Now, give every single little piece of your heart to the Lord, and He will begin the mending process. You will survive, times will get better, and you will, with the grace of God, be able to help others with the gift of God's love.

Love: A Variation on a Theme

If I live in a house of spotless beauty with everything in its place, but have not love, I am a housekeeper—not a homemaker.

If I have time for waxing, polishing, and decorative
achievements, but have not love, my children learn
of cleanliness—not godliness.

Love leaves the dust in search of a child's laugh.

Love smiles at the tiny fingerprints on a newly clean
window.

Love wipes away the tears before it wipes up the spilled
milk.

Love picks up the child before it picks up the toys.

Love is present through the trials.

Love reprimands, reproves, and is responsive.

Love crawls with the baby, walks with the toddler, runs
with the child, then stands aside to let the youth
walk into adulthood.

Love is the key that opens salvation's message to a
child's heart.

Before I became a mother I took glory in my house of perfection. Now I glory in God's perfection of my child.

As a mother there is much I must teach my child, but
the greatest of all is love.

Jo Ann Merrell

Love's Homework

As I said at the beginning of February's *Love* month,
Love isn't love until you give it away. You can actually have
"love homework." I assign myself love homework every so
often, to make sure my love skill isn't getting rusty. Give
yourself some love homework this month. Assign yourself
the task of loving someone you don't really like. I don't mean
that you make yourself her best friend, but determine (make
a decision of the will) that you will be obedient to Christ
and love her, in spite of her shortcomings. God will bless
you for that. God will take the animosity and hostility that

you had before for that person and replace them with the patience and forgiving attitude that comes with a transplant of God's love. Give yourself one love assignment each day, such as those detailed in the poem below, and you will end February just brimming over with love.

YOUR LIFE WILL BE RICHER—IF

On this day: You will make an effort to:
Mend a quarrel.
Search for a forgotten friend.
Dismiss a suspicion and replace it with trust.
Write a letter to someone who misses you.
Encourage someone who has lost faith.
Keep a promise.
Forget an old grudge.
Examine your demands on others, and vow to reduce
   them.
Fight for a principle.
Express your gratitude.
Overcome an old fear.
Take two minutes to appreciate the beauty of nature.
Tell someone you love him.
Tell him again.
And again.
And again.

AUTHOR UNKNOWN

The Power of Love

I recently heard a story that illustrates the power of a parent's love. A young woman whose child was pinned beneath her car, in her desperation to save the little one's life, raised the car sufficiently to allow him to escape. The load she lifted was far beyond normal human capability.

This sudden surge of supernatural strength occurs often. We are told that a chemical, known as adrenaline, on such occasions is infused into the blood, and provides the added strength. But there has to be a stimulus—something to trigger the glands—for this to happen. And this stimulus is what?

Love, of course. Love unleashes the greatest power under heaven.

I feel as if I know you, as you sit reading this book. I know I haven't met you all personally, but I still know you. How is that possible? Because I have been where you are! I know what it is like to lose a son in war—our son died in Vietnam. I know what it is like to lose a child unexpectedly—another son was killed by a drunken driver. And I know what it is to have my heart broken by a child—another son is living a homosexual lifestyle. So, you see, I do know just how you feel and that is why I can honestly say that I love you. I love you and have compassion for you, for the hurt, bewilderment, and pain you are going through right now. And I love you for what God is going to do in your life, mending your broken heart, putting the pieces back together, stronger than ever before. Maybe you need only a snippet of new elastic to pull yourself together—or the heavy-duty ribbed material. Whichever it is, love will help you get it *all* together.

Love unleashes the greatest power under heaven.

Because I have been there, splattered on the ceiling of panic, and because God has rescued me from that desperation, I can love each and every one of you who are in various stages of disintegration and restoration. I *know* God will help you. I *know* God will heal you. I *know* that there is hope. I have been there, I have been restored, and I have read the end of the Book—everyone *will* live happily ever after someday. "Love has a hem to her garment, / That trails in the very dust; / It can reach the stains of the streets and lane, / And because it can, it must."

February is our month of love. Take God's comfort blanket of love, wrap it snugly around you, and enjoy the warmth and protection it offers. With God's love, you can face and go through anything! Nothing comes into the life of a Christian without first passing through God's filter of love.

March

The Spade of Adversity

Happy March to all of you! I kept thinking about some of you back in the world of snow and ice. Here's a little suggestion: make snowballs and freeze them to give away in July. This might give you something to occupy your time—and give you something else to think about instead of the turmoil you're in right now over your children, because you probably feel all s-t-r-e-t-c-h-e-d out!

In California during the winter it is often 85 degrees; it's difficult to think of some of you back there in snow and ice. I have been thinking about bittersweet times and wanted to share with you some thoughts about memories and how God removes the sting, and time does allow us to remember the good, while painful memories seem to fade away like water-colored pictures in the rain.

A Warm/Cold Memory

Growing up in cold, wintry Michigan as I did, I think of snow falling, pure and white. We used to gather clean snow to make bowls of "snow ice cream," which is just simply adding nuts and raisins to sugar and snow. We had to eat it lickety-split before it melted. Icicles were fun, too. How neat it was to suck them into sharp points.

Making snow angels was another game we loved. We would fall back into the snow, making a deep imprint with our bodies. Then we would brush our arms and legs up and down, in and out, to make beautiful wings and robes. The trick was to stand up without ruining the "angel" imprint in the snow. Bundling up with fuzzy snowsuits and black rubber galoshes with metal clasps down the front seemed a small price to pay for all the fun we had. We'd come inside to drape our wet mittens and hats over the hot-air register, and drink hot chocolate to warm up our insides.

The next day we'd start all over again, bundling up to race our Flexible Flyer sleds down nearby hills. Sometimes we'd even use a round, metal tray or a cardboard box for excitement. Somehow, when I remember those times in Michigan, all the bad things that really happened to me seem faded, while the good happenings are as sharp in my memory as if they happened yesterday. I know one time I stuck my tongue on a metal railing, and it froze. I know several times I got chapped hands and frostbitten toes. But the pain associated with living in such a harsh climate seems removed from my memory now.

This is also what happens when time passes for parents whose children have caused them tragedy and heartache— perhaps the toughest kinds of pain there are. After the storm is over, there are bittersweet memories. After the first few months of shock and panic, some of the pain is drained off and healing begins. You begin to feel better for longer periods of time. You can go for a few hours and not be consumed by thoughts of your wayward child. Then, pretty soon, you can survive a whole day without anguish. That is when you know you are going to make it after all!

Just Being There

What we mothers have to recognize is that it is *all right* to hurt—hurt is a measure of the love we have invested in someone else. There is risk involved with love, and, too often, heartache. But the alternative is a life of gray and dullness. Love doesn't have to be profound, or educated, or dazzling. It just has to be there, steady and sure, even in the bad times. The following story illustrates this perfectly.

The Right Words
Her husband was in intensive care, and I was her friend. I didn't feel like going out in the cold of the night to be with her at the hospital. She even told me on the phone, "You don't have to come," but the reason I went was because of what she didn't say: "I need you."

The hospital seems awfully impersonal—white walls and old magazines in the lounge. There she was, looking so small and alone. She was so glad to see me, and then the tears she had bottled up just overflowed. What are the right words to say in a situation like that? What words of wisdom or Scripture should you recite? Well, I learned an important lesson that night. Sometimes God's wisdom doesn't use words! And so . . . I started to cry with her and there we both were, hurting and comforting each other in the middle of the night in a hospital with a good man who was dying.

The years have come and gone since that night, but somehow the Scripture, "weep with them that weep"

(Rom. 12:15 KJV) came alive for me that night, and has continued to remain alive in my life because sometimes the right words are no words at all.

The Eternal Lighthouse

March is generally cold, gray, and seemingly lifeless. Whether you are actually reading this in March, or on a sunny July day, your life *feels* like it's March. I hope this chapter will give you some encouragement that as bad as anything can become, God is that much better at turning it around for good, happiness, and life. When we have problems in our lives which seem so often to have no reason, and we lack any understanding of them, we have to rely completely on the lighthouse of God's direction for our lives and the rock of Christ's salvation.

We don't have all the answers. Some days I wonder if we have *any,* yet I know that when we throw up our hands after trying fruitlessly to make sense out of all this, we can only cling to *Him,* and know that we don't *have* to understand. Deuteronomy reminds us, "The secret things belong to the Lord" (29:29 NIV). Nothing comes into our lives until it first passes through the will of God. He has promised never to leave us or forsake us. Trusting Him is all we can do to carry us through the times when we flounder and see no way ahead of us to go on. This story will help you remember that God's will is our lighthouse, and His salvation is our rock.

Think of a ship at night, with its lights blinking. The captain sees another light in the distance, and he also sees a collision is inevitable. He sends out an emergency message which says:

"Emergency! Collision inevitable! Change your course ten degrees to the south!"

The answer comes back from the light in the distance:

"Emergency! Collision inevitable! Change your course ten degrees to the north!"

The captain of the first ship gets a bit hot under the collar and he sends back the same message, adding,

"I am a captain!"

To which the light in the distance replies:

"Emergency! Collision inevitable! Change your course ten degrees to the north. I am a third class seaman!"

The captain of the first ship is now furious. He sends out his previous message, adding,

"I am a battleship!"

And the answer comes back from that light in the distance:

"Emergency! Collision inevitable! Change your course ten degrees to the north! I am a lighthouse!"

We do have a lighthouse that never moves or changes: the will of God. And the rock that lighthouse stands on is Jesus Christ. Remember this story of the lighthouse and find some encouragement. Thank God for His lighthouse, a shelter from every storm of life!

Trial by Fire

We cannot always escape the bad times in life. Life is not always fair. There is suffering, sorrow, and pain. Right now, in your grief over what your child has done or what has happened to him or her, it seems that the pain will never end. You feel that *nobody* could know how badly you feel—that the sunshine will never enter your life again. Anything seems better than what you are going through right now. Grief and mourning are a necessary part of growing through the hard times. Through your suffering, God will help you to recover and will give you something positive out of it all. You who have endured the stinging experiences are the choicest counselors God can use! Remember, I've been there, too. In the midst of your grief, just hang on to the idea that this too will pass, and God will use it for good.

Here's an illustration to help you see the value in suffering. A bar of iron worth $2.50, when wrought into a horseshoe, is worth $5.00; if made into needles it is worth $175.00; if into penknife blades, it is worth $1,625. If it's made into springs for watches, it is worth $125,000. What a "trial by fire" that bar must undergo to be worth this! But the more it is manipulated, and the more it is hammered and passed through the heat, beaten, pounded, and polished, the greater its value.

Drain the Pain

I do need to note here that while acknowledging your pain and going through the valley of sorrow is necessary, there is no reason to prolong your stay in the valley any longer than necessary. Sometimes we get so used to suffering that we seem to be working at suffering! We become experts at depression. We craft our despair into a real work of art. That's not healthy, and it's not the way out of the pits! Determine today that you will suffer long enough to acknowledge the pain of your situation, but not so long that you get comfortable in grief.

The light of Christ is waiting just around the corner, waiting for you to ask for change and recovery.

How can you begin to climb out of the pit? One way is by throwing out the garbage you might be harboring to feed your misery.

We know that secrets are to sickness as openness is to wholeness. Drain the pain by sharing with another. Open up all the anger and allow the cleansing of God to bring refreshment to you. I love the idea of dumping the garbage in your mind and making room for thoughts that are honorable, right, pure, and lovely (Phil. 4:8). Memorize Philippians 4:8 to help you think on the good things, and dumping the garbage will be easier.

Another reason we often stay in a state of perpetual depression after severe trauma is that we think we are all alone. We know that we don't have the strength alone to survive, and we don't think there's anybody else who will help us. We are so nearsighted in our own preoccupation with grief that we fail to see God's hand in our situation. I don't care how dark your life is, the light of Christ is waiting just around the corner, waiting for you to ask for change and recovery. Even when we don't think we see anything positive in our circumstances, God's plan is quietly unfolding behind the scenes.

Real Parental Love Is Like God's

The love a parent has for a child should be a reflection of the love God has for each of His spiritual children. That's a love that can be hurt. That's a love that can cause pain. That's a love that can suffer, but can't be turned off. I know as a parent you would be willing to carry your hurting child over the hard times in his or her life, just as the Lord carries us through our hard times. That kind of love is precious—don't throw it away just because times are rough right now. One dad expressed eloquently the power of parental love:

"One day a father was talking to a friend about his son, who had caused great heartache. The friend said, 'If he were my son, I would kick him out.' The father thought for a moment, then said, 'Yes, if he were your son, so would I. But he is not your son; he is mine, and I can't do it.' " Don't give up your love for your child—put it in God's care and trust God for the healing. Make a copy of the following poem and tape it up where you can see it every day. It will remind you that God's love never fails and yours shouldn't either.

To One in Sorrow

Let me come in where you are weeping, friend,
And let me take your hand.
I, who have known a sorrow such as yours,
Can understand.
Let me come in—I would be very still
Beside you in your grief;
I would not bid you cease your weeping, friend,
Tears bring relief.
Let me come in—I would only breathe a prayer,
And hold your hand,

For I have known a sorrow such as yours,
And understand.

GRACE NOLL CROWELL

Pastor, teacher, and author Chuck Swindoll has developed this theme of sharing sorrows beautifully in his ministry. I have quoted extensively below from a sermon he gave one time which had a profound effect on my views concerning sorrow. There is hope for the downtrodden, and the deepest despair doesn't last forever!

Finding a Refuge

Let me get painfully specific. Where do you turn when the bottom drops out of your life? Or when you face an issue that is embarrassing, maybe even scandalous? Like:

- You just discovered your son is a practicing homosexual.
- Your mate is talking about separation or divorce.
- Your daughter has run away . . . for the fourth time. You are afraid she is pregnant.
- You've lost your job. It's your own fault.
- Financially, you've blown it.
- Your parent is an alcoholic.
- Your husband is having an affair.
- You flunked the entrance exam or you messed up the interview.
- You're in jail because you broke the law.

What do you need when circumstances puncture your fragile dikes and threaten to engulf your life with pain and confusion?

You need a shelter. A listener. Someone who understands.

But to whom do you turn when there's no one to tell your troubles to? Where do you find encouragement?

Without preaching, I'd like to call to your attention a man who turned to the living Lord and found in Him a place to rest and repair. His name was David.

Cornered, bruised by adversity, and struggling with a low self-esteem, he wrote these words in his journal of woes:

> In you, O LORD, I have taken refuge;
>   let me never be put to shame;
>   deliver me in your righteousness.
> Turn your ear to me,
>   come quickly to my rescue;
> be my rock of refuge,
>   a strong fortress to save me.
>   PSALM 31:1–2 NIV

Failing in strength and wounded in spirit, David cries out in his need for a refuge. The Hebrew term for *refuge* speaks of a protective place, a place of safety, security, and secrecy. He tells the Lord that He—Jehovah God—became his refuge. It was in Him the troubled man found encouragement.

Discouraged people don't need critics. They hurt enough already. They don't need more guilt or piled-on distress. They need encouragement. They need a refuge, a place to hide and heal, a willing, caring, available someone.

You can't find one? Why not share David's shelter? The One he called "My Strength, Mighty Rock, Fortress, Stronghold, and High Tower." David's refuge never failed. Not even once. And he never regretted the times he dropped his heavy load and ran for cover.

Neither will you.

You will find Him to be, just as He promised, "a very present help in time of need."

There is another dimension in all this that is easy to overlook. Sometimes the Lord directs us to become places of shelter and hope for others. Have you ever thought about being a refuge for someone else? Few roles are more gratifying, but in order to be a refuge for someone else, you need to be loving, compassionate, and accepting. Christians, we need each other! And that means we need to care for each other by being touchable, approachable, vulnerable, available. There's an old Swedish proverb which says, "Shared joy is a double joy. Shared sorrow is half a sorrow."

People of refuge share themselves through life's extremities. They open their hearts and arms to others. They double joys and halve sorrows simply by sharing both.

Finding a refuge . . . isn't that what we are all doing? Where do the wounded ones turn? So few out there are committed to helping restore others in pain, but instead many pass by with a shrug, wrapping around themselves their cloak of smug comfort, happy that what has happened to *us* hasn't happened to *them*. People who hurt as we hurt need a place to cry, a person to care, the security of intimate friends who will share our hurt. There are only a few lights to help the wounded when the bottom has dropped out.

You can begin your own healing by being a refuge for someone else. You can do for others what you need for yourself. Open your heart to someone else, even when you are in pain yourself. Together you can encourage each other and pray for each other. Sometimes we are seekers of refuges and be-ers of refuges at the same time! In this process of healing and becoming which we are all in, let us reach out and help others find that place of comfort, pointing others to the one shelter of God's care, a refuge to a wounded one.

My gift for your March of despair is a twofold thought: get rid of the garbage of bitterness that is contributing to your depression; find the Lord's refuge, from which you can be a refuge for someone else. God knows and God cares, and remember, too:

IT'S FRIDAY... BUT SUNDAY'S COMING

It's Friday   Jesus was nailed dead on a cross
    . . . but Sunday's Coming
It's Friday   Mary's crying her eyes out 'cause her baby Jesus is dead.
    . . . but Sunday's Coming
It's Friday   The disciples are running in every direction like sheep without a shepherd.
    . . . but Sunday's Coming
It's Friday   Pilate's strutting around, washing his hands 'cause he thinks he's got all the power and the victory.
    . . . but Sunday's Coming
It's Friday   People are saying, "As things have been, so they shall always be. You can't change anything in this world."
    . . . but Sunday's Coming

It's Friday   Satan's doing a little jig saying, "I control the whole world."

. . . but Sunday's Coming

It's Friday   The temple veil ripped from top to bottom—the earth shook—the rocks split and tombs opened. The centurion screamed in fear; "Truly he was the Son of God!"

. . . Sunday's Coming

It's Sunday   The angel, like dazzling lightning, rolled the stone away, exclaiming, He is not here! He is risen!

It's Sunday—It's Sunday—It's Sunday

April

Stick a Geranium in Your Hat

That new elastic you inserted so carefully, threading its way by means of a safety pin—it's holding!

Growing in the Valley

April is promises—April is a good month. It is hope. It is promise. It is newness . . . signs of spring: couples walking hand in hand in the park, jumping rope, jacks, marbles, baseball, neighbors calling across fences, housewives hanging out winter clothing to air. April is mist on the hilltops, rain on the roof, the smell of fresh-turned earth. It is violets, flaming azaleas, gardeners putting out pansy plants. April is dandelions, buds on the lilacs, the shiny green of new leaves, boxwood fragrant in the warming sun. April is watercress along the edges of streams, tiny green paintbrushes on the tips of evergreen sprigs, seedlings reaching up from neat rows in flats. April is rakes, forks, spades, and lawn mowers on the sidewalk in front of the hardware store. It is rain on the weekends, mud on the kitchen floor, and dirt and grass stains on the knees of blue jeans. It is storm windows coming down, screens going up, sparrows carrying bits of straw up under the porch eaves. April is the great stirring, the doorway to May, which is the most gracious month of all!

We all have to endure troubles in life. Some of us have sickness and pain, others may go along with just common irritations and then—*whammo!* Tragedy strikes. We all find ourselves in the valley of despair sometimes. But you all know that I believe we *grow* in the valley, because that is where all the fertilizer is! So learn to welcome the valley times, and see all the growth in character that comes from them.

Stick a Geranium in Your Hat

Recently I developed a neat idea someone suggested to me: "Life isn't what you want, but it's what you got, so stick a geranium in your hat and be happy!"

That is so true. We can decide if we will be happy in life, or if we will let troubles sink us, keep us down under the fertilizer, never growing above it to the mountaintops.

We can choose to gather to our hearts the thorns of disappointment, failure, loneliness, and dismay in our present situation. Or we can gather the flowers of God's grace, boundless love, abiding presence, and unmatched joy. I choose to gather the flowers. So find yourself a geranium and stick it in your hat. Decide you want the flowers, and not the thorns in life.

This month's message to you is: *Be Happy!* I hope you all will enjoy the silliness which comes with April Fools and the hope of spring!

Laughing Is Like Jogging on the Inside!

A Variation of Murphy's Law
(anything that can go wrong—will)

A day without a crisis is a total loss.

The other line always moves faster.

Leakproof seals—will.

Fail-safe solutions—aren't.

The repairman will never have seen a model quite like yours before.

Not until you finish walking to work will you discover your dress is caught in your panty hose.

The light at the end of the tunnel is the headlamp of an oncoming train.

Not-So-Famous Last Words

Many have experienced the confusion of traffic accidents and have tried to summarize exactly what happened in a few words or less on insurance or accident forms. The following quotes were taken from these forms and were eventually published in the *Toronto Sun,* July 26, 1977.

Coming home, I drove into the wrong house, and collided with a tree I don't have.

The other car collided with mine, without giving warning of its intentions.

I thought my window was down, but found out it was up when I put my hand through it.

I collided with a stationary truck coming the other way.

A truck backed through my windshield into my wife's face.

A pedestrian hit me and went under my car.

The guy was all over the road. I had to swerve a number of times before I hit him.

In my attempt to kill a fly, I drove into a telephone pole.

I had been driving my car for four years, when I fell asleep at the wheel and had an accident.

I was on my way to the doctor's with rear-end trouble, when my universal joint gave way, causing me to have an accident.

As I approached the intersection, a stop sign suddenly appeared in a place where no stop sign had ever appeared before. I was unable to stop in time to avoid the accident.

To avoid hitting the bumper of the car in front, I struck the pedestrian.

My car was legally parked as I backed into the other vehicle.

An invisible car came out of nowhere, struck my vehicle, and vanished.

I told the police I was not injured, but on removing my hat, I found that I had a skull fracture.

I was sure that the old fellow would never make it to the other side of the roadway, when I struck him.

The pedestrian had no idea what direction to go, so I ran over him.

I saw the slow-moving, sad-faced old gentleman as he bounced off my car.

The indirect cause of the accident was a little guy in a small car with a big mouth.

I was thrown from my car as I left the road. I was later found in a ditch by some stray cows.

The telephone pole was approaching fast. I was attempting to swerve out of its path when it struck my front end.

I was unable to stop in time, and my car crashed into the other vehicle. The driver and passengers left immediately for a vacation with injuries.

The accident was due to the other man's narrowly missing me.

In order to avoid a collision, I ran into the other car.

I remember nothing after passing the Crown Hotel until I came to and saw police officer Brown.

There were plenty of onlookers but no witnesses.

My car had to turn very sharply because of an invisible truck.

The accident was entirely due to the road bending.

The witness gave his occupation as that of a gentleman, but it would be more correct to call him a garage proprietor.

The other man changed his mind, and I had to run into him.

I told the idiot just what he was and went on.

If the other driver had stopped a few yards behind himself, it certainly would not have happened.

I heard a horn blow, and was struck violently in the back. Evidently a lady was trying to pass me.

Three women were talking to one another, and when one stepped back and another stepped forward, I had to have an accident.

The Tate Family

We'd like you to meet some members of our center. All of them share the same last name.

First there is old man Dic Tate, who wants to run everything, while his cousin Ro Tate tries to change everything. Mrs. Agi Tate stirs up plenty of trouble with the help of her husband Irri Tate. Whenever there is a new project suggested, Mr. Hesi Tate and his wife Vege Tate want to wait until next year.

Then there is Mr. Imi Tate, who wants our center to be just like the one he visited last year in Newtown. Mr. Devas Tate provides the voice of doom, while Mr. Poten Tate just wants to be a big shot. But there is also Mrs. Facili Tate, who is most helpful when there is work to be done. Mr. Cogi Tate and his wife, Medi Tate, always want to think things over and are usually positive in their ideas.

And finally, there is the black sheep of the family, Mr. Ampu Tate, who has cut himself off completely from the center, which is his own business. We're sure you have met some of the Tate family in your place of work, too.

This little piece about spring rains reminds me so much of April where I grew up, that I want to share it in this month:

God Washed the Earth

The wind whipped the tree branches, forcing them lower and lower. The lightning lashed at the sky. Though it was midday, the darkness was near complete. Birds huddled in the trees. A small child cried at a thunderclap that shook the earth. A dog barked excitedly and shook as lightning licked across the horizon.

Then the rain came. Washing down over the earth. Drenching all those who were caught out in the summer storm. Rivulets of water ran down the streets forming puddles along the sidewalks. Waves of rain ran down from the heavens. The air awoke in the downpour. Swishing in and out among the trees and bushes. Flowing up and down and blowing out across the lawn. The air was clean. A deep breath of fresh air, sweet-smelling, met with everyone venturing back outside to watch the ground suck up the water thirstily. The parched lips of the streets welcomed the wetness. Refreshed, the world breathed a sigh, for God had washed the earth.

VICKIE BLACK

THEN LAUGH

Build for yourself a strong box,
    Fashion each part with care;
When it's strong as your hand can make it,
    Put all your troubles there;
Hide there all thought of your failures,
    And each bitter cup that you quaff;
Lock all your heartaches within it,
    Then sit on the lid and laugh.

Tell no one else its contents,
    Never its secrets share;
When you've dropped in your care and worry
    Keep them forever there;
Hide them from sight completely
    That the world will never dream half;
Fasten the strong box securely—
    Then sit on the lid and laugh.

BERTHA ADAMS BACKUS

You Know You've Had a Rough Day When . . .

- You drive into the repair shop, and your mechanic starts singing "I'm in the Money."
- The deduction from the raise you just got is so big that you have to take a second job to replace the money you lost.
- You tell the salesclerk you are looking for a pot holder and she directs you to the girdle department.
- You are contemplating lining the rim of your boss's coffee cup with Super Glue.
- You can't avoid the speeding ticket by flirting or crying because the police officer is a woman.
- You eat an entire batch of brownies because you feel that "you deserve it."
- After you drive home from work, you rip the "Have a Happy Day" bumper sticker off your car.

You Know It's a Bad Day When . . .

- You turn on the morning TV news, and they're displaying emergency routes out of the city.
- Your boss tells you not to bother taking off your coat.
- The bird singing outside your window is a buzzard.
- Your horn gets stuck when you're following a group of Hell's Angels on the freeway.
- You put both contact lenses in the same eye.
- Your pet rock snaps at you.
- You call your answering service, and they tell you it's none of your business.
- Your income-tax check bounces.

- You wake up to discover your water bed has broken, and then you remember you don't have a water bed.
- Your bar of Ivory soap sinks.

Restoring a Relationship

It seems the months fly by quickly, and now winter is over and we are into spring. Easter is just a few days away. Holidays always bring out-of-town visitors to our home in Southern California, and we have some great times of sharing with relatives and friends. Sharing does help drain the pain parents go through with wayward children. We do a lot of sharing at our weekly meetings for parents. At our meeting in March, we had a really happy surprise: Our son Larry, who had disappeared into the gay life, the one I wrote about in *Where Does a Mother Go to Resign?* came to our meeting! And he was carrying a huge bouquet of flowers for me. He brought two friends along with him, and they all shared during the meeting. Hearing Larry speak about the growth that has taken place in the past few years, and the insights he has learned, which, in turn, can help others mend their relationships, really was encouraging to the parents at our meeting. There were lots of hugs and tears, lots of emotional responses, and I wanted you to know that I am rejoicing because there has been a restoration in our relationship. The word *restore* means to "pop back in place," and that's what we had been waiting for.

This has brought so much hope for other parents. To see anger and bitterness and hardness disappear, to be replaced by a gentle spirit and overflowing love, is exciting! We are all on the journey to wholeness. Some are farther down the road, some have stopped at resting places, and some have even detoured. But none of us has arrived! I just wanted to share this exciting news with you, and it's *not* an April Fool joke! Some of you might be dubious, but this really happened! No joke!

When you are low down, with arms dropping down and bent knees, then read Hebrews 12:12: "Wherefore lift up the [drooping hands] and the feeble knees" (KJV). Have you heard the song "Garment of Praise," with the words, "Put on the garment of praise for the spirit of heaviness, Lift up your voice to God. . . . Lift up the hands that hang down, Lift up the voice now still."

Weed, Feed, and Seed

In April the ground is warm and thousands of bulbs open, working their way up through the soil toward the warm sun. But you know, other things grow, too. We call them *weeds*. Some are fragile and easy to get rid of, but others have deep roots and tough stems. If you are a good gardener, you have to get the weeds out to protect the flowers. Remember the nursery rhyme, "Mary, Mary, quite contrary, How does your garden grow?" How about the garden of your mind? You can let weeds sprout and multiply, let them choke out new life. Or, you can cultivate the garden of your mind and watch your days bloom one by one.

You can dig out those roots of discord and bitterness. Cultivation is vital. Even a well-weeded garden can produce plants that don't look right if they have not been fed. Weed it, seed it, and then feed it. Fertilizer is plant food, and faith is soul food. Without fertilizer, your garden cannot flourish, and your spirit cannot grow without faith. Underfed plants droop. So do people. Are you drooping today, arms down and spirit drooping? Check what you are being fed in your mind and your spirit. Maybe some weeding is necessary right now, some cultivation, digging out some roots of weeds that are stopping fresh growth. Clean up your spiritual garden today, along with adding that much-needed elastic. As you insert the fresh piece, be sure there is enough stretch to include *mirth!* We *do* believe in mixing fun with our recipe for life. He who laughs, *lasts!* So put guffaws, snickers, giggles, and titters high on your priority list. Sincere laughter is a powerful tonic for weary, battered souls.

Some Favorite Funnies

Excuses, Excuses . . .

A friend from Oklahoma City who was visiting here over the Easter holiday brought me a reprint of a column called "Looking at Language" by Richard Lederer, which I thought was funny and decided to use. The following are excuse notes parents actually sent to school.

- My son is under the doctor's care and should not take P.E. Please execute him.
- Mary could not come to school today because she was bothered by very close veins.
- Please eckuse John being absent on Jan. 28, 29, 30, 31, 32, 33.

- Please excuse Roland from P.E. for a few days. Yesterday he fell out of a tree and misplaced his hip.
- Please excuse Jimmy for being. It was his father's fault.
- Please excuse Sarah for being absent. She was sick and I had her shot.
- John has been absent because he had two teeth taken off his face.
- Chris had an acre in his side.
- Please excuse Gloria from Jim today.
- Lillie was absent from school yesterday as she had a gangover.
- Sandy and I won't be in school a week from Friday. We have a funeral to attend.

A Further Favorite Funny

We all know about the prodigal son, but *this* little ditty was composed by Phil Kerr and is called "Melody in F." I think you will enjoy reading it. Get by yourself and read it over *out loud.* Then practice it on someone you know—you both will be laughing by the time you get finished with it!

Feeling footloose and frisky, a feather-brained fellow forced his fond father to fork over the family farthings.

He flew far to foreign fields and frittered his fortune feasting fabulously with faithless friends. Fleeced by his fellows in folly and facing famine, he found himself a feed-flinger in a filthy farmyard.

Fairly famishing, he feign would have filled his frame with foraged food from fodder fragments.

"FOOEY! My father's flunkies fare far finer!"

The frazzled fugitive frankly facing facts, frustrated by failure, and filled with forboding, flew forthwith to his family.

Falling at his father's feet, he forlornly fumbled, "Father, I've flunked." He fearlessly forfeited family favor.

The farsighted father, forestalling further flinching, frantically flagged the flunkies to fetch a fatling from the flock and fix a feast.

The fugitive's fault-finding brother frowned on fickle forgiveness, but the faithful father figured filial fidelity is fine and so the fugitive was found! "What forbids fervent festivity? Let flags be unfurled, let fanfares flare."

MORAL: Father's forgiveness formed the foundation for the former fugitive's future fortitude!

PHIL KERR

Spatula Seeker

Since April is for April Fools, thank you for allowing me to share some fun things to cheer you up. Let me tell a little story on myself to show you how funny "ordinary" things can be. As I've mentioned before, our ministry for hurting parents is called Spatula Ministries, since parents who are devastated by their kids' actions hit the ceiling and need to be scraped off with a big spatula! Well, I am always on the lookout for cheap plastic spatulas to use for illustrations at meetings where I speak, and to give away to new people.

I was in a local drugstore last week and I saw a sales-girl kneeling down, sorting out a large box of kitchen utensils, among them brightly colored plastic spatulas—for only fifteen cents each! The spatula I had been using at meetings looked more like a kitty litter scooper—so often they break, or get lost in the shuffle, that it seems as if I am always looking for a nice, solid spatula to demonstrate for someone. Seeing these lovely ones, I excitedly asked her if I could sort through all the utensils with her and pick out all the spatulas from the other stuff. I found about thirty of them. How wonderful to have so many! There were enough to last me the whole year. Good-bye to the kitty litter scooper!

Gleefully I loaded myself and my shopping cart down with all these shiny plastic spatulas sticking out the sides and bottom of the cart. When I paid for them I said, "I am so happy to buy all these nice cheap spatulas. Do you know how hard it is to find such nice ones so cheap?" The girl just looked at me, and swooped them all up, stuffing them into a sack. I figured it was more fun *not* explaining what I wanted them for. As I went through the checkout, I turned to her and said, "Well, it's whatever turns you on!" I am sure that the drugstore personnel figured I had just been let out of the Home for the Bewildered!

You see, for me, going home, thinking about what the salesgirl must have said to her co-workers, made me laugh. So do whatever makes *you* laugh—tasting Christmas on old pine branches, buying spatulas by the bushel, or hibernating with old *I Love Lucy* reruns. Find yourself some way to flatten out your pain. Talking it out helps so much. That's why Spatula Ministries has been such a winner—letting people talk out their grief and pain, encouraging them to ventilate their anger, to get it out, to examine their feelings and express their heartache, and *then* to introduce *joy* into their lives. Having a sense of humor is what has saved me from the pits. I still get there, but I don't *stay* there. You have to learn to develop a sturdy ladder to climb out of the pits—one rung at a time, probably, and laughter and humor are the bottom rungs on which to start the upward climb!

Become a Child Again

How long since you did some fun, childlike things? Simple things like eating watermelon on top of the water tower at midnight? Or jumping into piles of autumn leaves? Or gathering big armfuls of lilacs and bringing them to friends so their homes would smell like spring? The value of fun lies in the spirit of it, whether it is climbing windmills, or marching in a parade, or going up on the down escalator. Break out of your little plastic mold and become a *real dingy* person (not *din-gee,* but *ding-ee*), even if people think you are fresh out of a rubber room. Laughing helps. It's like jogging on the inside.

Laughter and humor are the bottom rungs on which to start the upward climb!

Look for ways to enjoy your day, however small or trivial. Even finding a convenient parking space may bring joy. Begin to look for fun things. They are there. People can be fun (funny too). Sit on a bench sometime and just watch them. (Don't look for ones who look like the child you've lost or who has disappointed you.) Just look at people, and marvel at how each one is a unique reflection of God's creative diversity. Look at a field of flowers and see flowers, not weeds. (If you have any secret special ways of relieving your own depression, do let me know.)

80

Mary Lou's Rx

I called my special friend, Mary Lou, who has been struggling with us in Spatula Ministries for a couple of years. She was so far out when I met her, you couldn't even see her. She's just been naming and claiming and standing on the Word, pointing to a verse and demanding all the bonds be broken, and refusing to accept the problem in her son. She has a marvelous sense of humor, and we have laughed and cried together. I have learned a whole lot from her about coping. She told me today that when she really feels down, she has a special way of being lifted. (I was expecting some spiritual gem!)

Look at people, and marvel at how each one is a unique reflection of God's creative diversity.

Instead, she said, "I get out an old Shirley Temple movie for the videotape player, and get a box of chocolate chip cookies, and lie down. For a couple of hours, I just escape it all!" So get yourself some old Shirley Temple movies on videotape, and maybe this will work for you. Maybe you could substitute Ry-Krisp for the other cookies so you don't have to *roll* out the door!

The Post Office Caper

This is the month of fun, so I guess I'll let another one of my escapades out. I went to the post office today. The doors to get in don't push in, you have to pull them to get in. Now, this isn't hard, unless you are loaded down with tapes and mail, as I usually am. So, I just stood there with both arms loaded, waiting for some kind soul to either come out (so I could catch the door on the rebound), or for someone to go in ahead of me and hold the door.

Today the landscapers for the city were clipping the evergreens, which are in front of the post office, and with stacks of the greenery lying around, the smell was pungent with pines. It actually smelled like Christmas in April! So when a kindly old gentleman came along and opened the door so I could get in, I smiled, and instead of thanking him, I said, "Doesn't it smell just like Christmas around here?" He sort of halfway smiled and went on to get some stamps or something.

On the way out of the post office, he was just behind me, and I reached down, picked off a tiny piece of the evergreen, and put it in my mouth, and then I turned to him and said, "You know, it even tastes like Christmas around here!" The startled look on his face was worth a million dollars to me! But you see, I *do* love pines, and it *did* smell like Christmas, and the tiny piece I chewed on did *taste* like Christmas. See what *fun* I had, savoring that smell and taste that everyone else was too busy for?

Are you a stretched out mom? Laughter will stretch your life—the right way.

May

The Door of Hope

It's May already! We talked about the importance of beginning again, unconditional love, overcoming adversity, and the role of laughter in assuring that your fresh elastic is getting it all together. In May, the word for you to *hug* close to you is hope—because Mother's Day always brings to mind memories of former happy days. Perhaps this particular Mother's Day will be one of heaviness and separation for many of us.

This is from Ruth Graham's *Sitting By My Laughing Fire,* and is my cherished thought for you on Mother's Day:

> She waited for the call
> that never came;
> searched every mail
> for a letter,
> or a note,
> or card,
> that bore his name;
> and on her knees
> at night,

and on her feet
all day,
she stormed Heaven's Gate
in his behalf;
she pled for him
in Heaven's high court.
"Be still, and wait,"
the word He gave;
and so she knew
He would
do in, and for,
and with him,
that which she never could.
Doubts ignored,
she went about her chores
with joy;
knowing, though spurned,
His word was true.
The prodigal had not returned
but God was God,
and there was work to do.

FROM *SITTING BY MY LAUGHING FIRE* BY RUTH BELL GRAHAM, COPYRIGHT © 1977; USED BY PERMISSION OF WORD BOOKS, PUBLISHER, WACO, TEXAS.

There are so many of us who have prodigal kids who are bringing heartache and pain to us. But read this over, and remember *there is work to do,* and *God will do what He promises.* He always goes after the prodigal. We have to get on with the business of life, not get stalled on the tracks and run over by the train of doubts.

One verse from the Bible which is especially meaning-ful about hope is Proverbs 13:12: "Hope deferred makes the heart sick; but when dreams come true at last, there is life and joy" (TLB).

Hope Is a Rag Doll

Today I was in a shopping mall, poking around in a gift and card shop, dreading the upcoming Mother's Day with all the heaviness it brings to me and so many other parents I know. I was thinking about hope and how to instill it in others. It seems so many are wading through deep waters, almost sinking with despair this month.

Suddenly, I saw a darling little rag doll, and on the box she came in were these big, bold words: HELLO! MY NAME IS HOPE! Inside, on her blouse, was printed: "I'M HOPE!" How kind of the Lord to let me stumble onto that bit of encouragement. After all, who can describe hope to anyone? Hope is that light at the end of the tunnel, when all around you is black. (But that is sort of vague, really.) Actually, what is written above, about God being *God*, and there is work to do—*that* is hope translated into life. *That* is what you and I have to do, though spurned, which is how most of us with wayward kids feel right now.

Roots and Wings

There are two things we can give our children. One is roots, and the other is wings. Yes, the first is easier to give than the last. If only there were a magic button to push when our kids become adults, so we could relinquish them easily, give them wings, and have confidence they will fly right and soar, and then come home at their pleasure, to share their freedom with us.

In reading *The Friendship Factor* by Alan McGinnis this week, I loved the portion where he tells us that children are not properties to own and rule over. They are *gifts* to cherish and care for. Our children are our most important *guests.* They enter into our home, ask for careful attention, stay for a while, and then leave to follow their own way. How terrific if we could all remember to let go when we sit on the panic button, frozen and paralyzed, when our little chicks don't do what we want them to do. They have followed their own way (which is not our way *or* God's way). How wonderful if we *could* train up a child and then let him go!

Leaving the store with my newly purchased doll tucked snugly under my arm, I hurried home, thoughts about hope filling my mind. Yes, as long as our child is alive, there is *hope!* Even if it is not happening right now, and our hearts are sick because our hope is deferred, put off, or postponed; we cannot give the final score on a life until the game is over. And it is not over with us yet.

Let Go

The problem is that many parents try to play Holy Spirit for their kids. We try to bring conviction to them, but instead we bring condemnation. It is the job of the Holy Spirit to *convict.* That is why many kids become resentful when parents try to force God on them. We have to give them to God, and then take our hands off. It is like wrapping a package up and putting on a label, and then being able to send it, without our special directions of where to go, but letting God put the address on the label, or on that life. Can you love your child and pray for him and let God do with his life what He wants to do? Minus your instructions? Can you be content to train up your child and then let him go? If you can do that, you can enjoy this Mother's Day, knowing that, though spurned, your child is God's property, and God always goes after the prodigal! Remember that God's love surrounds you with a golden band of hope and promise!

Water-Color Memories

Although Mother's Day is very painful for many of you, take this time to remember the funny and joyous things that are a part of mothering, too. I've used this piece to pick my spirits up on days when I've felt miserable as a mother. See if they help you, too.

You Know You Are a Mother When . . .

- Your son comes home from college and has rented a U-Haul trailer to carry the dirty clothes he wants you to wash.
- You have an assortment of seventeen handmade clay ashtrays, and no one in your family smokes.
- Your three-year-old calls you into the bathroom to retrieve the Star Wars soldier out of the toilet.
- Your freezer is packed with the twenty-seven boxes of Girl Scout cookies your daughter couldn't sell to anybody else.
- You are in a clothes store and your teenage daughter keeps calling you by your first name, so nobody will suspect that she is shopping with her mother.

- You catch yourself singing the theme song from the *Mr. Rogers' Neighborhood* show.

Mother's Day is a time when our children are supposed to appreciate what we have done for them, but so often when our children are walking alone, away from the family (and usually away from the Lord), we worry that they will never understand how we tried to raise them in the best way we could, even with mistakes. The following letter was written by a brokenhearted mother the day after she learned her daughter was a lesbian. It says so explicitly what hundreds of parents feel. I know that reading this, you parents will feel it is your own heart that is writing these feelings:

God, yesterday I cried. You probably cried too, because we both love her so much. If I didn't love, it wouldn't matter so much. I wonder why she left us, God, You and me? Especially You. I've tried to be a good mother to her.

Remember, God, those long years ago that she came to live with us? How proud her father and I were to have her become part of our family. We were just bursting with joy and anticipation for all the wonderful moments we would have together. Remember, how we lost her one day, just to find her up in the tree. And remember all the cute things she would say. How much love there was in our family then. She had some favorite times, like sitting on the back porch eating her mayonnaise sandwiches and potato chips, looking over the pond in the quietness of the midday. How I wish I could bring just one moment of that time back to enjoy once more. But that is gone forever.

Then the day she started to school. Her first grade was such a happy time, having such a devoted teacher that first year; being elected favorite of her little class and getting her sock monkey, George, from the school party. Those days filled with Bluebird meetings, friends coming to visit her, birthday parties, etc. That was about the time I started back to college. The day she and [her dad] came into the bedroom, where I had shut the door with instructions to be left alone, stating that they had voted for me to quit college, because she couldn't see me enough. I was so touched I almost cried.

Then she grew into junior high age. A good little basketball player and my pride and joy, as I would go to the games and watch her play. She would ride with me, as I went to school. That was funny the day she got my box purse and carried it to class, and left me with her little one just like it. That was such a nice summer you allowed our family to have in Florida, when she was still in junior high. Remember how worried her dad and I were when the plane she was coming in on was late, and finally, when it arrived, I saw her dad wipe away the tears from his eyes—tears of relief that everything was okay after all. God, remember that day we were at the beach and we found the sea turtle's eggs. That was such an exciting experience! Oh, if only I could recall a small portion of that day just to enjoy once more.

It was during this period that she came to know You, Lord. Such a dedicated little Christian I've never seen before. She was so burdened for the lost friends, trying so hard to win someone to You. She did her best to witness to [a friend], and yet the girls of the neighborhood would leave her out of their group. She kept her little chin up though. High school came with the band, a boy, sports, and her singing in the youth choir. Her specials with the guitar were just beautiful. Thank You, God, for the youth leader to be a blessing at that time in her life. And then came graduation. How beautiful she looked that night; a night of mixed emotions for me—happiness that she had come so far, and yet sadness that my role as mother to her needs was almost ended. Remember the rose we so lovingly gave her that night—all of our best wishes and love went with it.

Thank You, God, for all the happy moments we have had with her. As I look back, I realize I did not take time to enjoy them as I should have, until they slipped away forever into the eons of time. But thanks, anyway, for the memories. God, I wish I could have been a better mother, perhaps using better judgment in time of problems. But, God, You know that I have loved my daughter more than she will ever know, and I did my best.

Yes, God, I cried yesterday, and today—and I'll probably cry tomorrow. Even after the tears have ceased to flow from my eyes, my heart will forever yearn for her to return to us, You and me. Because God, I know You are crying too.

WRITTEN BY A MOTHER WHO IS HEALING . . . SLOWLY

The Heart of a Mother

Washington Irving, who lived nearly two hundred years ago, knew a lot about the love mothers have for their children. Having just read the piece above, reading this from Washington Irving will serve to give you another perspective on how we feel toward our children.

There is an enduring tenderness in the love of a mother to a son, that transcends all other affections of the heart. It is neither to be chilled by selfishness, nor daunted by danger, nor weakened by worthlessness, nor stifled by ingratitude. She will sacrifice every comfort to his convenience; she will surrender every pleasure to his enjoyment; she will glory in his fame, and exalt in his prosperity; and if adversity overtake him, he will be the dearer

90

to her by misfortune; and if disgrace settle upon his name, she will still love and cherish him; and if all the world beside cast him off, she will be all the world to him.

May is the month for Mother's Day, and try as we will, it brings with it more pain to some of us than pleasure. But we are taking Philippians 4:8, thinking on things that are pure, right, and uplifting!

Resignation Refused

Anyway, there is no place to resign. You are in it forever. A mother's love goes on and on, even when her child is grown and gone. God planted a mother's love so deep that the roots of it go deep and far into our hearts. There is no place to resign, quit, or escape, so you might as well kick back, throw it out of gear, and enjoy the day! If your kid is "out to lunch," and forgets you, find another one, and hug him, love him. Find another lonely kid around and use your imagination. Don't let anyone rob you of the fun which belongs to you. So what if you don't get a card or flowers or even a call! Send your child a note telling him (or her) you love him even if you don't get any return. Keep sending out love messages, even if you feel you are trying to hug a porcupine! Keep sharing your heart. Keep on planting and watering seeds. Keep sending out the love message and planting love seeds in your family. Don't expect much back and you won't be disappointed, but keep on planting seeds. You are not in this alone. There are thousands of mothers trying to make this day meaningful, so do it by planting your love in someone else! I know it works for me, and it will for you, too. Be glad for your mother's heart; your love is special, as Dianne Lorang shows so well.

THE LOVE CHAPTER FOR MOTHERS

If I talk to my children about what is right and what is wrong, but have not love, I am like a ringing door-bell or pots banging in the kitchen. And though I know what stages they will go through, and under-stand their growing pains, and can answer all their questions about life, and believe myself to be a devoted mother, but have not love, I am nothing.

If I give up the fulfillment of a career to make my chil-dren's lives better, and stay up all night sewing cos-tumes or baking cookies on short notice, but grum-ble about lack of sleep, I have not love and accomplish nothing.

A loving mother is patient with her children's immaturity and kind even when they are not; a loving mother is not jealous of their youth, nor does she hold it over their heads whenever she has sacrificed for them. A loving mother does not push her children into doing things her way. She is not irritable, even when the chicken pox has kept her confined with three whining children for two weeks, and does not resent the child who brought the affliction home in the first place.

A loving mother is not relieved when her disagreeable child finally disobeys her directly and she can punish him, but rather rejoices with him when he is being more cooperative. A loving mother bears much of the responsibility for her children; she believes in them; she hopes in each one's individual ability to stand out as light in a dark world; and she endures every back-ache and heartache to accomplish that.

A loving mother never really dies. As for home-baked bread, it will be consumed and forgotten; as for

92

spotless floors, they will soon gather dust and heel marks. And as for children, well, right now toys, friends, and food are all important to them. But when they grow up it will have been how their mother loved them that will determine how they love others. In that way she will live on.

So care, training, and a loving mother reside in a home, these three, but the greatest of these is a loving mother.

DIANNE LORANG

Make this Mother's Day a good, refreshing day. Remember back to when Mother's Day meant breakfast in bed, handmade, sticky "presents" from kindergartners? We seem to have forgotten some of those earlier, happier days!

Whether you are reading this during the calendar month of May (when the pain of separation from your child on Mother's Day is especially sharp), or during some other time of sorrow when you are missing your child and evaluating your past commitment as a mother, these short lines are meant to encourage you that, in spite of the pain, mothering was worthwhile. You *do* make a difference in your child's life, even if he or she is denying you right now.

> Youth fades, love droops,
> The leaves of friendship fall;
> A mother's secret hope
> outlives them all.
>
> OLIVER WENDELL HOLMES

Hang In There

Hang on to the *hope!* We know that when we get to the end of the rope, we tie a knot and hang on, but do you know what that knot at the end of the rope is called? It is *hope.*

That's the possession of each Christian because we have a solid basis for hope. We have the assurance that as long as He is with us, we are more than conquerors. Jesus is *our* hope. He is God's gift of grace to us. When we say that a person or a situation is hopeless, we are slamming the door in the face of God.

> Hope springs eternal, and is held by the bedrock of God's love.

Sometimes the circumstances of life leave us so devastated that hope is buried in the black pit of pain. But even then, there is the foundation of hope that remains to be built on again. It is that light at the end of the tunnel. Hope springs eternal, and is held by the bedrock of God's love.

Clearing the Cobwebs

May is here. It's a time for cleaning out drawers, putting fresh paper on shelves, dumping collections of junk we have squirreled away. Clever housekeepers keep an unused dust mop to shake out the front door. Then they shake the real one out the back door at night. Every so often, we should dig out the corners. It's a good idea, even when it does make the middle of the room a mess. (I finally did it the other day when I noticed a gopher hole.) In the summer you can blame dust on open windows; in winter on the furnace. If someone points out a cobweb, quickly say, "Oh, you mean William's science project?" May is the month for throwing open the doors and clearing away the cobwebs.

Once a year, the story goes, the town drunk made a pilgrimage to the church to settle the score with God. And every year he stumbled down the aisle, praying, "Lord, clean out the cobwebs, clean out the cobwebs." One old lady, exasperated by the drunk's routine, interrupted him on his trip to the altar by standing and praying, "Lord, forget the cobwebs. *Kill that spider!*" We must clean the cobwebs in our lives, but getting rid of the spiders is top priority, too. May is the time for taking inventory on our corners, setting things in order in our lives as well as in our homes.

Yes, May is our month of *hope* as parents. This is how *The Living Bible* renders this special verse from Hosea 2:15: "I will . . . transform her Valley of Troubles into a Door of Hope." That is an obscure verse, one that I have not heard anyone preach or teach on before. In the valley you learn so much about endurance and patience. When you are down there so low, you can think about the verse in Hosea: that the Valley of Troubles can be transformed into a Door of Hope!

Healing Our Scars

I received this letter from a doctor in Texas who recently lost his brother in a tragic suicide. I know it will bring hope to you as a parent.

. . . the past few weeks have been emotionally packed for my parents and many of the feelings of grief and anxiety have been similar to those felt by you many years ago. I thank you for sharing the comfort you received with us, and I pray God continues to comfort you. The wounds are fresh for us now, but you have helped us to begin that healing process, and I know as all physical wounds heal with the Lord's healing power, that these will also heal in time. But I also know that when a wound does heal, it leaves a scar as a reminder of the change from the original area of smooth skin. The scar holds and it is as strong as original skin, but we are able to see that something has occurred inside at one time. Barb, I'm grateful God gives us healing and scars so we can grow and learn more about Him, and that we may remind ourselves daily of the wounds that once were very sensitive and painful, but are now nothing but reminders as scars.

Author Joseph Bayly answers this way when questioned about suicides: "We don't have all the answers, but we know he went out to meet a just and merciful God." How good that we can leave it in God's hands, and know that He has all the answers in His time for us. "[He gave us] beauty for ashes, the oil of joy for mourning, the garment of praise for the spirit of heaviness" (Isaiah 61:3 KJV).

Hope Is Plain Honesty, Too

Hope doesn't always have to be sunny. Sometimes hope is *just plain honesty.* Sometimes when we are so down that we don't think there even is an up, honest expression of our feelings is as close to hope as we can get. One of our darling gals who comes down to our ministry and helps me with shuffling papers and mail has been in such a depression for many months. She is so cute and so *honest* about her feelings that she just bumps along and says what she feels and usually brings down the house, laughing.

Last week she told me that when she sees the bumper stickers that say, **I'd rather be sailing,** or **I'd rather be fly-**

ing, she wishes she had one that says, **I'd rather be DEAD!** That was so honest of her, and so much like her feelings, that I had to commend her for being so transparent. It is true that we *all* wish we were dead sometimes, and could escape all the pain and tragedy we have been going through for so long. But it is *because* of the suffering, the pain and loss and separation, that we grow. Maybe this book will let you know that your feelings are honest and normal—but not forever. We are in the furnace of pain to become gold, not to melt away to nothing.

Here is a great message on how we have to give our children our best, and then let go and let God. Use it this month to give you *hope* for recovery.

IT'S YOUR MOVE, DAUGHTER ...

I gave you life
   but I cannot live it for you.
I can teach you things
   but I cannot make you learn.
I can give you directions
   but I cannot always be there to lead you.
I can allow you freedom
   but cannot account for it.
I can take you to church
   but I cannot make you believe.
I can teach you right from wrong
   but I can't always decide for you.
I can buy you beautiful clothes
   but I cannot make you lovely inside.
I can offer you advice
   but I cannot accept it for you.
I can give you love
   but I cannot force it upon you.
I can teach you to be a friend

but I cannot make you one.
I can teach you to share
    but I cannot make you unselfish.
I can teach you respect
    but I can't force you to show honor.
I can grieve about your report card
    but I cannot doubt your teachers.
I can advise you about friends
    but I cannot choose them for you.
I can teach you about sex
    but I cannot keep you pure.
I can tell you the facts of life
    but I can't build your reputation.
I can tell you about drink
    but I can't say NO for you.
I can warn you about drugs
    but I can't prevent you from using them.
I can tell you about lofty goals
    but I can't achieve them for you.
I can let you baby-sit
    but I can't be responsible for your actions.
I can teach you kindness
    but I can't force you to be gracious.
I can warn you about sins
    but I cannot make your morals.
I can love you as a daughter
    but I cannot place you in God's Family.
I can pray for you
    but I cannot make you walk with God.
I can teach you about Jesus
    but I cannot make HIM your Savior.
I can teach you to OBEY
    but I cannot make Jesus Your Lord.
I can tell you how to live
    but I cannot give you Eternal Life.

AUTHOR UNKNOWN

Never Give Up!

We can never give up hope with our children. God is not finished with them or us yet, and our hope can sometimes mean the difference between a relationship that fades away to nothing and a restoration between parent and child.

There are some parents who have done what they could to bring up their children "in the nurture and admonition of the Lord" (Eph. 6:4 KJV), only to have them reject not only what they have been taught, but their parents also. These are the *exceptions* to Proverbs 22:6.

Do you have a friend with such a child? If so, what have you done? Have you been judgmental, critical, gossiping, and perhaps smug because your children are staunch believers, wholly committed to the Lord? This little poem by Ruth Bell Graham speaks vividly to us on the subject:

> They felt good eyes upon them
> and shrank within—undone;
> good parents had good children
> and they—a wandering one.
>
> The good folks never meant
> To act smug or condemn,
> But having prodigals
> just "wasn't done" with them.
>
> Remind them gently, Lord,
> how You
> have trouble with Your children,
> too.

FROM *SITTING BY MY LAUGHING FIRE* BY RUTH BELL GRAHAM, COPYRIGHT © 1977; USED BY PERMISSION OF WORD BOOKS, PUBLISHER, WACO, TEXAS

We must always remember how God hates sin and yet is so tender and compassionate toward the sinner. How often we fail to make that distinction!

HE'LL SEE THEM HOME

Don't despair so of your children,
  God will bring them to the fold—
Because He died to save them,
  They're special to the Lord.
He knows how much you love them,
  He loves them even more.
As long as you hold on in prayer,
  He'll not close the door.
Even now He sees your tears,
  And He whispers tenderly,
Of Love that conquered all—
  That all men might be free.

So lay them at His altar,
  Let go and leave them there—
God will be faithful to your trust,
  He won't withhold His care.
His hand will ever nurture,
  No matter where they roam—
And He won't be satisfied
  'Til He sees them safely home!

JOYCE HENNING

Yes, we *can* hope even when we don't see any tangible results in our relationship with our child. We don't know what God might be doing for him or her. We don't know how God is using what we try to do for him or her, even when we don't see the results. I know the situation of a young woman, a lover of flowers, who had set out a rare vine at the base of a stone wall. The rare vine grew vigor-ously, yet the woman noticed that it did not bloom despite the lavish care paid to it day after day. One morning, as the young woman stood disappointedly before it, her invalid neighbor, whose backyard was adjacent to hers, called over and said, "You can't imagine how much I enjoy the blooms of that vine you planted." Very quickly the woman looked, and on the other side of the wall she saw a mass of blossoms. The vine had crept through the crevices and had provided beauty for her neighbor.

I hope the strength and power of that message isn't lost. Often we cannot see the fruits of our work, and so think our work has been in vain. In God's service somewhere, all of our efforts, whether visiting, telephoning, praying, doing a kind deed, making a meal, or whatever—all of our acts of love bear their fruit, and some heart receives their blessing and joy.

Christopher Morely said, "If we discovered we had only five minutes left to say all we wanted to say, every tele-phone booth would be occupied by people calling other people to stammer that they love them." That's real hope!

RSVP

Christ said,
"Come unto Me,
All ye that labor
And are heavy laden
And I will give you rest."

These
Were just beautiful words
To me—no more—

Until I realized
That my name
Was on the invitation.

Hope seems to persevere even when we are at our most "down times." Happiness and hope are so closely intertwined that it seems as though if we just grab onto that little bit of hope, it pulls us up out of the pit enough to remember that happiness is possible.

Trouble into Treasure

My prayer for you for May is that you will feel the comforting arms of God around you, giving you hope for the future. God can take your trouble and change it into treasure. Your sorrow can be exchanged for joy, not just a momentary smile, but a deep, new joy. It will be a bubbling experience of new hope, with brightness in your eyes and a song in your heart. In the midst of the darkness, you will learn lessons you might never have learned in the day. We all have seen dreams turn to ashes, ugly things, hopeless and terrible experiences. But beauty for ashes is God's exchange. You may offer yourself to God and ask for a spirit of praise, so your whole being will be restored. Tears and sorrow come, but each time God will be there to remind you that He *cares*. Romans 8:28 means, "God causes all things in our lives to work together for good." Flowers can even grow on dung heaps, and compost makes great gardens.

A song says that if tears were promises and heartaches were gold, I'd have all the money my pockets would hold. We know the iron crown of suffering precedes the golden crown of glory. That is a comfort! You are not alone. There are thousands like you who are trying to find some relief from nights of crying and pain. Give your son or daughter to God, and then focus on getting *your* life together. Keep learning about your child's problems. Sin is pleasurable only for a season. Keep in mind that *you are not responsible for what you cannot control.* Remember, God only called you to be faithful; He did not call you to be successful! Genuine healing is a process, and takes us a long, long time. It takes time for the deep hurts to be resolved.

> **Give your son or daughter to God, and then focus on getting your life together.**

Beautiful Day, Isn't It?

The day had started out rotten. I overslept and was late for work. Everything that happened at the office contributed to my nervous frenzy. By the time I reached the bus stop for my homeward trip, my stomach was one big knot.

As usual, the bus was late—and jammed. I had to stand in the aisle. As the lurching vehicle pulled me in all directions, my gloom deepened.

Then I heard a deep voice from up front boom, "Beautiful day, isn't it?" Because of the crowd, I could not see the man, but I could hear him as he continued to comment on the spring scenery, calling attention to each approaching landmark. This church. That park. This cemetery. That firehouse. Soon all the passengers were gazing out the windows. The man's enthusiasm was so contagious I found myself smiling for the first time that day. We reached my

> Finally, brothers, whatever is true, whatever is noble, whatever is right, whatever is pure, whatever is lovely, whatever is admirable—if anything is excellent or praiseworthy—*think about such things.*
>
> PHILIPPIANS 4:8 NIV,
> ITALICS ADDED

stop. Maneuvering toward the door, I got a look at our "guide": a plump figure with a black beard, wearing dark glasses, and carrying a thin white cane. Incredible! He was *blind!*

I stepped off the bus, and suddenly, all my built-up tensions drained away. God in His wisdom had sent a blind man to help me see—see that, though there were times when things go wrong, when all seems dark and dreary, it is still a beautiful world. Humming a tune, I raced up the steps to my apartment. I couldn't wait to greet my husband with, "Beautiful day, isn't it?"

Definition of a Winner

To have hope is to be a winner. Even when you are last in the race, even when all of your friends' children are models of perfection and spiritual holiness while yours have bitterly disappointed you, you can be a winner if you have *hope!*

BE A WINNER

The winner is always part of the answer.
The loser is always part of the problem.
The winner always has a program.
The loser always has an excuse.
The winner says, "Let me do it for you."
The loser says, "That is not my job."
The winner sees an answer for every problem.

The loser sees a problem for every answer.
The winner sees a green near every sand trap.
The loser sees a sand trap near every green.
The winner says it may be difficult but it is possible.
The loser says it may be possible but it is too difficult.

AUTHOR UNKNOWN

You can survive and be a winner! Remember the old song: "Hallelujah, we win, I read the back of the book, and we win!" God will never let you sink under your circumstances. He always provides a net. His love always encircles you. God always keeps His promises. You will get through this and you will be back in the flow of life. You can win this battle of depression. And when you are a winner, then you can reach back and pull along some other suffering person who needs to be told he can be a winner!

Be an Optimist

Someone told me that her favorite Scripture verse was, "And it came to pass." I looked at her rather quizzically, and then she laughed and added, "Just think. All this could have come to *stay!*" While we are in the passing-through stages, we have to derive comfort from others who have survived. Be a survivor, and help someone else!

This is from *Today's Christian Woman,* and is of such hope to those of us who wonder sometimes if there is hope *anywhere.*

Down with Pessimism

I am one of those people who never takes an umbrella in the morning unless it's pouring rain at the time. I cheerfully ignore road signs, such as "Men Working—Expect

Delays," and I refuse to worry about the deficit, acid rain, or the decline of SAT scores. Things will get better.

I'm an eternal optimist who expects interest rates to go down, the Russians to reform, my ship to come in, and the sun to shine on my picnic.

So I immediately reacted the other day when I heard my mother sigh, "I wouldn't want to have to bring up children in this day and age."

I suspect that Socrates' mother said the same thing and that senior citizens ever since have sung the refrain. I mean, is the world really in any worse shape than in the days of Attila the Hun, the Dark Ages, or the Inquisition? Are there really any new problems under the sun? Unisex and uppers and cholesterol and Central America notwithstanding, I tend to believe that only the faces of the problems have changed.

Recently, however, I've begun to wonder if Mother isn't right—as usual. With, for example, our nuclear capability to reduce everything between Minsk and Missouri to radioactive rubble, can anyone but a naive optimist have any faith in the future?

Studies reported in *Psychology Today* show that many kids fear they won't have a future. They grow up thinking they may not grow up. As one youngster put it, "I have now accepted the fact that there quite possibly will be an 'end of time.'"

No one knows just how these anxieties affect kids. But it doesn't take a world-class shrink to figure out that, as one put it, "It's hard to expect kids who feel that way to work hard in school, develop deep relationships, or do anything that has a future element to it."

To compound the problem, it appears that parents are paralyzed on the issue. Parents who are fond of warning, "Kids are pretty smart, you kow. They pick up everything," avoid discussing the nuclear issue.

The bomb isn't the only cause of pessimism in this generation. The sweet and sour fruits of technology which have drastically changed our lifestyles, our relationships, and even our health, have also skewed our thinking about the future.

Parents themselves have lost a little faith in the so-called American dream that their children will be materially better off than they were. A *Washington Post ABC News* poll revealed lower expectations on the part of parents for their children's financial future.

One psychiatrist, according to the *Psychology Today* article, counsels parents to give their children "hope."

Hope in what? Hope in history? Hope in some mathematical odds against a disaster? Hope that some paranoid, tin pot, Ruler-for-Life of Whazzooland won't get hold of a big bomb and begin the ultimate nuclear holocaust?

This counselor doesn't say, but having hope sounds an awful lot like the groundless optimism that prompts me to leave my umbrella at home.

The difference is crucial. My optimism stems from something in my experience, personality, genes, whatever—I'll never know. My Christian hope is based on the sure knowledge of God's love and managerial ability.

Yes, Mother may have a point, but I still believe we can have hope. We can have hope when a child runs away or when a marriage unravels or when bankruptcy threatens.

The hope that is in us in Jesus Christ, come detours or deficits or dictators or any other unimaginable adversity, makes it possible for us to live full and satisfying lives.

So let it rain!

RON WILSON

Hope/Miracles

Hope and miracles are almost synonymous. Sometimes our hope seems to invite God to do a miracle in our lives.

Sometimes our hope gets a much-needed boost from a miracle sent just for that purpose. In a way, hope in the midst of despair is a miracle in itself:

THERE'S A MIRACLE AHEAD!

There's a miracle ahead! I know!
   My mortal eyes see but the present hour
But God bends low and whispers to my heart,
   "My promises are true, they never lose their power
To change each needy soul—
   each sin-sick one—
To that sweet image of My blessed Son!"

Oh, yes, I've wept and prayed, and broken on the wheel
   Of pain not dreamed by my most loving friends,
But I was so remiss in failing to look back
   To recollect the miracles that He did send!
So, troubled one, there's a miracle ahead!
   Be not crushed by doubts that can destroy—
Look up, believe God's precious Word, and lo!
You'll find one day, despair will turn to joy!

When we have hope, we are showing that we *trust* God to work out the situation. As a parent, especially one whose child has caused heartache, it's sometimes hard to have hope and trust God. But trust is the only way we're going to make it through and be a part of God's marvelous plan for our child. We cannot force our child to change and restore our relationship—*but* we can hope for God's best, and trust in God's plan.

No matter how much I might tell you that hope helps, or no matter how much God may be trying to work with your attitude to help you, you will not begin to change

How to Change a Flat Attitude

A wrong attitude is like a flat tire: It needs to be changed before you can get anywhere.

Step One: Pull over and stop. You must stop and admit that your attitude is wrong and must be changed. As you do this, try to specifically pinpoint what it is about your attitude that is wrong, and why you have this attitude.

Step Two: Jack it up off the ground. Leave that attitude to God in prayer. Let Him help you set up some reasonable goals for yourself in changing your attitude. The more you trust and depend on Him to keep you from falling into the same old patterns, the sooner you will see the change.

Step Three: Remove it and replace it with a new one. Replace that wrong attitude with a positive attitude. Positive attitudes come from meditating on the Scriptures and on the goodness of the Lord. (See Philippians 4:8.)

Step Four: Lower it back into place. Get ready to put that positive attitude into practice. Do a Bible study on the new attitude and seek specific guidelines for using it.

Step Five: Now start the engine and take off! Continue on to your destination, "But be ye doers of the word, and not hearers only, deceiving your own selves" (James 1:22 KJV), and "Commit your way to the Lord, trust also in him, and he will bring it to pass" (see Psalm 37:5).

until you are *willing* to change your attitude. If you won't change your attitude, you won't begin to recover. This is so important that I've made a little illustration of "changing a flat attitude." It may be in light terms, but I'm deadly serious about the idea. If you are willing to change your attitude, you will have victory!

So remember May—the month of mothers, the month of hope. Your child is in God's hands—let Him take the burden of your sorrow and build victory through your hope! This isn't the end of your life; it's the beginning of your future!

June

Decorating Your Desert

Still have that stretched out feeling? Well, keep going, because June is our month to "decorate our deserts." I know that sounds kind of odd, but let me explain what decorating and deserts have to do with developing and practicing a positive mental and spiritual attitude as part of our recovery as parents.

After one of our ministry's parents' fellowship meetings, one of the fathers was telling us about his daughter's upcoming wedding. "She's making big plans," he said, "but the catch is, the wedding is going to be in the desert!" Then, with a grin, he threw up his hands and asked, "How do you decorate a desert?"

We all laughed, but on the way home, my mind was filled with ideas about deserts, and dryness, and streams in the desert, and finding refreshment, and mostly about decorating the desert places in our lives. These lines came to me:

A little love, a little trust
A soft impulse, a sudden dream,
And life as dry as desert dust
Is fresher than a mountain stream.

How to Start Decorating

How often have you had times in your life when you've felt you were in a desert, with nothing to give you refreshment, or had no comfort for your parched circumstances? It is at such times that we must learn how to decorate our desert, to realize that God has given us two hands—one to receive with and the other with which to give. We are not cisterns made for hoarding—we are channels made for sharing.

If you can put one touch of rosy sunset into the life of another, you should feel that you have worked with God. This is one way of decorating your desert, reaching out to comfort someone around you who is hurting. Can you, even in your desert place, reach down to *lift* another's load? This is a big step toward decorating your own desert.

The desert is hot and dry. You have problems galore that seem unsolvable. Yet, when you are with the Lord, it is as though you were given a cup of cool water, dipped from an ever-flowing stream. You drink as though you could never drink enough—and yet while you drink you are satisfied completely. He can give you springs of living water that will bubble up from within you like joy that is percolating from inside you and bubbling up to refresh others around you.

Have you ever been in the desert at night and seen the glistening stars twinkle brightly? They seem so much closer out in the desert, and the moon seems so much brighter and almost within your grasp if you reach out to touch it. All around us we can find sparkling jewels from God scattered in our dark places—if only we look for them. Can you find streams in your desert, and make places of oasis for others traveling through your sphere of influence?

See how many ways you can put color and life and water and contentment in others' lives.

Can you decorate a desert? See how many ways you can find to put color and life and water and contentment in others' lives, and you will find your desert will bloom—and so will you. As Psalm 107 reminds us, "He turned a desert into pools of water and the parched ground into flowing springs" (v. 35 NIV).

What Is a Joy Room?

One of my "decorated deserts" is what I call my "joy room." It's an oasis I turn to whenever I am down, and over the years it has been an oasis for countless parents who have shared its comfort with me. My Joy Room has encouraged me and so many others who have come to visit us, so let me tell you about it and pretend you are here for a sharing time with me.

We started out with just a *joy box,* which was a decorated shoe box with cartoons and fun things to pull me out of the pit, when I had no other outside help from complete despair. That joy box grew so large, we finally had to add a room onto our mobile home—so much joy and love flowed into us from friends all over the country.

It is a large room, about sixty feet long, with green carpeting and light walls. The door has a stained-glass window with a white dove etched in the middle. Walking into my joy room is like walking into bright sunlight. I like things that move, shine, and make noises, so there are lots of things like that. There is a plant which is a light—it comes on when you touch it on the leaves; a couple of scenes that move, on the wall, and a bird that sings and chirps when the sun hits it. There's a clown that laughs when you pull a string attached to his tie. Everything in the room has been given to me, most of it from parents whose grief I have shared and to whom I have tried to be a little oasis. Now they have learned to share a cool drink in the desert with me, too.

My joy room has all kinds of emotional "picker-uppers." There are balloons and rainbows; handmade plaques; pillows which have special messages on them; and several little handmade dolls with spatulas in their hands, reminding me that when I am splattered against the ceiling, I have faithful friends waiting to peel me off again!

The room has a miniature train set, and the little train actually rides along a track. We have some milk can stools equipped with tractor seats for comfort to sit on. There are stuffed animals, rag dolls, and catchy signs and plaques on every inch of the wall space. My Mrs. Beasley doll sits in a small rocker along with some other dolls dressed in handmade outfits. On one door is a motto which says, LOVE SPOKEN HERE.

There is no lock on the door to my joy room, so friends can come in anytime, sit in the huge puffy pillow recliner, and just enjoy all the cheer in that room. You have to be happy in the joy room, because there are smiling faces all around you, and little windup toys that move, and several music boxes that play bright tunes. The telephone there is a Kermit the Frog phone. It makes you laugh just to see him. He is bright green with red trim (and the phone works fine). I also have a multicolored balloon lamp, which looks like it came from a child's nursery, but I love it!

There is a jar of jelly beans and some other decorations on the shelves which are tempting, too. There is a large, stained-glass butterfly window on one end, and a sign on the door, saying, WHATEVER, LORD! It is such an accumulation of joy from all over. Everything in it was sent from loving hearts.

Sometimes I sit in my joy room, just to get a lift when things are getting me down, or when I'm tired and still have so much to do. Often I pray individually for the people who have been so warm and generous to send me special things as reminders of their love. And often I sit there and pray for the ones who aren't ready to share a cool drink in the desert yet, who are still hurting so badly that they need some help in decorating their deserts. If you are one of those hurting ones, take heart! I'm praying for you! And start decorating your desert right now. You will be amazed at the difference a refreshing drink in the middle of the desert makes.

My joy box pulled me through the rough days when I had nothing else going for me. I felt all alone in the dark pit. I didn't know then that others had been through it and had made it!

Collecting poems, cartoons, verses, and making myself look for joyful things brought me from where I was, so that now I can look back and remember it, but I am not there anymore. I learned to put on the garment of praise for that spirit of heaviness. I realize that it had come to *pass,* and not to *stay.* Healing takes time, but it comes.

Joy in Tin and Wood

So my word to you is get yourself a *joy box!* Decorate a shoe box and start today. Collect things from the newspaper, your favorite magazine, the Sunday comics. Start being a collector of joy. You will find it all around. Everyone has a special way of peeling himself (or herself) off the ceiling, and I have found that visiting a card shop is a good way for me to restore the joy that sometimes gets robbed around here. It seems like joy robbers are all around, but a trip to the Christian bookstore really restores me.

Start being a collector of joy.

What does it take for you? You'd better find some fast, inexpensive method to meet your own need for joy and humor in your own life. Without it, you are dead in your sorrow, with no hope at all.

At first you may have a shoe box for your "lifters"; then you may enlarge it to a basket, and then a barrel. Before you know it, you may have to add a room onto your home, just as we did, just to have a place large enough for all the joy!

Looking through your joy box, or sitting in your joy room, is a form of therapy, and even the clock seems to chime out the message, "I love you, friend, so very much!"

I feel I have earned my joy room, having come up from the black pit and now into life again. One of my joy ingredients is a little poem I memorized to remind me of the process needed to produce joy out of heartache. May I share these four lines?

> There is no oil without squeezing the olives,
> No wine without pressing the grapes,
> No fragrance without crushing the flowers,
> And no real joy without sorrow.

You don't have to be very sophisticated to find desert decorators. In fact, sometimes the less sophisticated you are, the easier it is to find joy in an ordinary day. Practice looking for joy, and you will be surprised at all the places you find it.

Defining Joy

Joy doesn't have to be expensive. You don't have to sell your family jewels (if you have any) to buy joy. Joy is thoughtfulness. Joy is caring. Joy is saying, "Thank You, God," for life. Let those around you who love you share joy with you. The oasis built in your desert by your family can be the best one of all.

Two of the best gifts I got last year were from people who loved me. The first was just a piece of tin, and the second was just a splinter of wood, but both brought me true joy.

The piece of tin was from our special son, Barney. He knew that when we moved from our old home to where we now live, what I missed the most was the sound of rain on the tin roof at our old house. I used to love listening to the rain on a winter afternoon, as I would sit and sip my tea, enjoying the coziness of our home.

One day our son brought me a big piece of tin, the kind mechanics use under cars. It was all ready, so I could put it on the roof. Now when it rains, I can enjoy the sound of the rain hitting that tin, reminding me of the warm home God has given me. It wasn't an expensive present, but it had all the meaning in the world.

Be a Lifter-Upper

The splinter of wood was from a dear friend, and it has a verse inscribed on it: ANXIOUS HEARTS ARE VERY HEAVY BUT A WORD OF ENCOURAGEMENT DOES WONDERS! (Proverbs 12:25 TLB). Talking to so many anxious parents each week, I used to feel drained after some sessions. But God used that gift to teach me that I should be a "spirit lifter," a light in the dark of night; a comforting hand on a troubled shoulder; or a guide to one who is lost. Most discouraged people do not need professional help; they need those little appreciations, approvals, or admirations that can lift their spirits and give them the courage to keep on coping with the nitty-gritty of life.

Joy from loved ones can be a simple and powerful encourager.

So you see, joy from loved ones can be a very simple and very powerful encourager. Recognize the joy those who love you are holding out to you, and think of how you can be a spirit lifter to someone else. It's all part of decorating your desert!

Let's talk a little bit more about being an encourager, to yourself and to others, when we feel drained. That verse from Proverbs helps me, and so has one very important principle I've seen work over the years.

People ask me, "How do you stand to listen to so many problems all day?" There are lots of answers to that question. Partly I'm helped tremendously by being able to refer people to good professional help in their area. But, all in all, if I can help people to develop a sense of humor, that is the best way to cope with all problems.

After you have given your problem to God, you can then sit back and expect Him to work on it. The only thing you can really do is to love your child who is in rebellion and pray for him, and then get to work on putting yourself back together.

Giving your burden to God is where the *faith* comes in, and *hope* is always in the picture, even if it is hope deferred. So many parents are so serious about their problems that they are unable to find anything that will bring joy or fun into their lives.

Fun Is Where You Find It

I have learned to find fun in unlikely places. Fun is a mystery. You cannot trap it like an animal; you cannot catch it like the flu. But it comes without bidding, if you are looking for it.

Recently I made a sad trip—by plane to Michigan for the funeral of a beloved aunt. As I boarded my return flight to California, I noticed a little girl, sitting all hunched up across the aisle from me. She looked so small and so afraid. The flight attendant told me she was traveling alone.

I thought, *Oh, well, the attendants will look after her.* I was busy going over the last few days . . . the funeral . . .

the many people who had grown older since I had last seen them . . . it was all very depressing. I knew the five-hour flight home would be my only time to be alone with my loss. I had no intention of entertaining a little six-year-old who evidently had never been on a plane before.

As the plane took off, I noticed that she shut her eyes tightly and clenched the seat belt with bone-white knuckles. I felt something inside me want to ask her to come sit by me.

When we were safely in the air, I asked the attendant if it was all right, and she replied, "Oh, yes! She has never flown before. Her parents have divorced, and she's on her way to California to live with relatives she's never even met before. Thank you for caring."

My "fun" started when the hostess came through with the complimentary beverages. Darling little Suzie with her dancing black eyes said she would have a 7-Up. I asked the hostess to put it in a fancy glass, with a cherry in it, because we were pretending we were special VIP ladies taking a super trip. Having 7-Up with a cherry in it in a fancy glass may not be your idea of fun, but to a six-year-old who had never had it that way before, it was great fun. We were off to a great start.

Our pretending went on, and I could see that I had missed so much in having all boys, never learning as a mother of a girl what little girls thought of. Suzie thought the luncheon on the plane was just like miniatureland. The tiny salt containers were a great joke. The tiny cup from the salad dressing was just for Munchkins. I had so much fun, enjoying with her child's eyes, all the goodies on our trays. We had our own special tea party. The little paper umbrella anchored in the dessert caused her to remark, "I got to see *Mary Poppins* once." I knew this was one of her most special experiences, and so we pretended that she was Mary Poppins. We kept her little umbrella, and Suzie had to learn to walk like Mary Poppins, with her toes sideways and holding the umbrella up just so. She did a great imitation!

Just taking Suzie to the little bathroom was an experience. She couldn't figure out how things worked. She wanted to know if the soap was so small because somebody had used it almost all up!

When we returned to our seats, the attendant gave us both coloring books and three crayons—blue, red, and yellow. So, together, we colored some puppies in the book red, made a yellow gypsy, and a blue ballerina. It was fun! She had lost her fear of flying, and we looked out on the cottony sea of clouds, talking about what fun it would be to walk on the clouds, holding our Mary Poppins umbrellas, and see how far we could go.

Then it was time to land. The hours had melted away. I had been a child for a few hours, playing her game, coloring her pictures, exploring her child's mind, seeing life through the eyes of a six-year-old. I had learned so much!

I will always remember that fun day, and when I eat on an airline flight, I always think of the "Munchkin" dinner Suzie and I shared that day. She got off ahead of me when we landed, and I rushed to try to catch up with her. I saw as she was swooped up into the arms of a grandmotherly lady with twinkles in her eyes. Suzie turned to me and said, "Look, Grandma, I am Mary Poppins!" She held her little umbrella up, turned her little feet sideways, and smiled a big smile of pure joy. The grandmother thanked me for looking after her, but *I* was the one who was taken care of that day!

It could have been a dreary, sad trip for me, lost in my own reverie of sorrow, but instead a little girl became a diamond of love and joy for me.

When life gets so heavy for you, and you wonder how you can cope with all the load, learn to put on the garment of joy for the spirit of heaviness, and fun is included in that garment of joy. Suzie turned my desert into a decorated place of joy. Look for that joy in your life, too. Don't settle for grouchiness and sorrow: settle for joy and happiness.

Eliminate the Grouch Box

Do you have a *grouch* box instead of a joy box? Throw it away and stuff your *joy box* full. Do you know how you can equip yourself to find decorations for your desert, and joys for your joy box? *By knowing that your sins are forgiven by Jesus Christ*—just because He loves you, and not because you deserve it.

Eliminate the *If Onlys*

So often as parents we blame ourselves for our kids' mistakes and tragedies. "*If only* I had been stricter," "*If only* I had given him more freedom," or "*If only* I had talked to her more," or "*If only* I hadn't badgered him so much with complaining." Nobody is a perfect parent, and there are not trial runs at parenting. We just love our kids and do our best—God doesn't demand anything more.

So stop blaming yourself for decisions your child has made. Accept God's forgiveness, and rejoice that straightening your kid out is His responsibility, not yours. A favorite verse says, "What happiness for those whose guilt has been forgiven! What joy when sins are covered over! What relief for those who have confessed their sins and God has cleared their record" (Ps. 32:1–2 TLB). You can have joy, you can beat your depression, you can decorate your desert. And in decorating your desert, you will be decorating yourself.

When I was in the depths of my own depression, I had my driver's license picture taken. I looked *horrible!* The picture that stared at me from my license for the next four years shocked me every time I looked at it. Then, as I began to get some joy back into my life, and started decorating my desert, I started decorating myself. Life came back into my eyes. They were no longer chronically puffy and red from endless tears. My cheeks turned pink instead of waxy sallow. And my sagging down-in-the-mouth lines stretched up into laugh lines. When I got my new picture taken, boy, was I happy! No more reminder of death-warmed-over each time I opened my wallet! I actually looked better and younger four years later than I had in my previous picture. See what decorating your desert with joy can do? And it's not nearly as expensive as plastic surgery! So get moving, and get joy.

> What happiness for those whose guilt has been forgiven! What joy when sins are covered over!
>
> Psalm 32:1

Here are twenty-five suggestions to help you get that joy and decorate yourself and your desert—fast!

Pamper Yourself!

25 Ways to Beat the Blues

Do you ever wake up feeling bored, depressed, lonely, or unhappy? Fortunately, those unhappy times can be turned around. On your next "bad" day, consider using some of these proven mood lifters:

1. Make a list of everything that is preventing you from being happy today. Consider postponing all negative feelings for 24 hours.
2. Make another list—this time of your blessings. Include everything good that's ever happened to you.
3. If you spend a lot of time watching television, decide today you will watch only one good program.
4. Declare a be-kind-to-your-body day. Enjoy a massage, facial, manicure, and/or new hairstyle.
5. Spoil yourself a little: Buy something you've always wanted.
6. Give your environment a face lift. It doesn't have to cost much. How about new dish towels for the kitchen, or some beautiful new bathroom accessories?
7. Take a walk through a park, or explore a new area. See how much beauty you can find along the way.
8. Eat foods high in Vitamin B. Avoid foods high in refined sugar or salt. Vitamin B foods (whole grains, fruits, vegetables, and meats) are especially soothing. On the other hand, refined sugar devours the B

complex vitamins, upsets your blood-sugar level, and predisposes you to nervousness. Salt increases irritability.

9. Give yourself at least one success experience today. It could be doing exercises you hate or completing an unpleasant task.
10. Lose yourself in a good book. Read anything by Erma Bombeck.
11. Buy a new plant or a bouquet.
12. Call two favorite people and tell them how much you love them.
13. Take a mini vacation. Get on a bus, plane, or train, and visit a place you've always enjoyed. Or go somewhere new and exotic. If money is a problem, check into a nearby hotel and play tourist for a day.
14. Get out an unfinished project and finish it.
15. Start a new project.
16. Clean and organize your environment. Attack your drawers, cupboards, and closets. Gather up photographs and put them in an album.
17. Do an anonymous good deed.
18. Write notes of appreciation to people who have been a special help or influence in your life.
19. Live out a daydream. A good how-to book that will spur you is *Wishcraft* by Barbara Sher and Annie Gottlieb (Viking Press, 1979).
20. Visit a friend you haven't seen in a long while.
21. Plant some favorite flowers.
22. Take a friend to lunch. Talk about the good things in the world.
23. Make up with an old friend.

24. Realize that having a good day is really your own choice.
25. Give everyone a smile.

At first you might think that list is childish, that you don't need twenty-five commonsense, insignificant ways to win over depression. But when you are in the midst of the black cloud, you can't see your way out by yourself. You need someone to hold your hand and guide you back out into the sunshine. Don't make fun of everyday things that can really be positive steps to restoration and recovery! Christian author Grace Noll Crowell knows this, and she's said it beautifully in this poem:

I HAVE FOUND SUCH JOY

I have found such joy in simple things;
A plain clean room, a nut-brown loaf of bread,
A cup of milk, a kettle as it sings,
The shelter of a roof above my head,
And in a leaf-laced square along a floor,
Where yellow sunlight glimmers through a door.

I have found such joy in things that fill
My quiet days: a curtains' blowing grace,
A potted plant upon my window sill,
A rose fresh-cut and placed within a vase,
A table cleared, a lamp beside a chair,
And books I long have loved beside me there.

We've pretty well covered what it means to decorate your desert, fill your joy box, and look for laughter all around you. In your calendar of recovery, June is your month to be constructive in your pain, to find an oasis in the desert of your hurt. With your trusty canteen of hope from May at your side, you should be able to strike out across the desert of your despair and find that oasis of joy. It's sort of easy to find joy in the midst of a hopeful situation, but now you are strong enough to find joy in the midst of frustration.

With God's Help ...

People hurt in so many ways, and there seem to be many joyless people. Even those of us who have deep and abiding joy which comes from the Lord can sometimes lose its evidence under all the garbage of life. Find your joy, and hang on to it. See God's care for you even in the small things in your life.

Now decorate your desert. Turn your sorrows into joy. Make a joy box today, and start to fill it with happiness from the Lord. There's not a lot of challenge in harvesting carefully nurtured hope—God can help you rise to the challenge of picking blossoms of joy from the midst of the thorns.

July

Living in Hurts Castle

Just a snippet of new elastic may be all you need to get you out of Hurts Castle. Let me explain:

July and the other summer months are vacation months, and if you live in Southern California, you know that July is also the month when you have the most out-of-state company. Everyone wants to stay with us when they come for Disneyland, Knott's Berry Farm, and the other Southern California attractions. A woman wrote me not too long ago, asking if she could see me when she was planning to be in Southern California, seeing "Hurts Castle." She was just picking herself up out of depression caused by her two rebellious teenagers, and I guess she didn't know the castle is *Hearst* Castle, not *Hurts* Castle!

Move Out

But "Hurts Castle" certainly does describe the dwelling place most of us prefer when we first are struck with what seems like a child's total failure at life. The hurt is there, but we should remember that we are just *visiting* Hurts Castle. We are *not* permanent residents. We cannot go back and unscramble eggs. There is no way to undo what has been done and play the "blame game" on and on. We have to start with what we have. We cannot change the past, but we can ruin a perfectly good present by blaming ourselves for past mistakes. We have all failed in many areas of our lives, but failing doesn't make us failures! We have to learn from our mistakes, and learn how to prevent them in the future. We cannot whip ourselves with a lash of remembered failures. Let's move out of our past failures, and starting with our scrambled eggs, learn how to make soufflés!

My prayer is that God will wrap you in His special comfort blanket and make you know He is in control of the situation. You are not alone out there. Just nestle in His arms. Enjoy the comfort of knowing He has it all in control: your broken heart, your wayward child, your complicated life problems. You might as well learn to enjoy the trip, because each day God gives us the grace for that day alone. You can make it, one day at a time. This short prayer from a hurting mother has given me comfort—I hope it comforts you, too.

A Mother's Prayer

Hurts

It seems that everyone hurts. All people hurt in some part of their life. I suppose that as long as there is sin, there will be hurts. Lord, give me strength today. Place within me the ability to cast my hurt onto you. You have already borne all of the hurt. You bore it on Calvary. You have fought the sin battle, and you won the victory. Because of Calvary, this victory is mine . . . Now . . . Today.

Have mercy and show your pardon and love to my child this day. Release him from the temptations that could destroy him. He is your boy. I want to remind you that I gave him to you. All rights to his life are yours, yet distractions are calling him from the world around him.

Forgive me my sins and overlook my mistakes. Bring to me your comfort. Relax all of the parts of my mind and emotions that are tense and burdened down with this great hurt.

Lord, as I trust you this moment for my own peace and assurance, I also trust you to care for his needs. I believe. I am singing your praises for the mighty work that you are about to perform in the life of one of my children.

No Parking

Those who are familiar with my ministry of "peeling" parents off the ceiling when they have wayward children know that my car is a Volvo with the license plate SPATULA. One day, some months back, I parked in a spot where I wasn't supposed to, and a man's loud voice boomed out at me, "Mrs. Spa-TOO-la, you aren't allowed to park there!" I started laughing, thinking I never had heard the word pronounced that way, but it reminded me that not all the world knows what Spatula Ministries is about! It made me think about the preacher who said he saw a sign that said, DON'T EVEN THINK ABOUT PARKING HERE. And it was signed by the Chief of Police. I could think of many people I have known through the years, parking in life's "no parking" zones. Here are some parking zones I've made up that should help you get out of Hurts Castle a little more quickly.

No Parking by Your Defeats. Everyone has had defeats in one area of life or another. Some have had bankruptcy and had to start over again. You may have had social failures and endured shame. Don't *park* by this sign. Move on to new opportunities in your life.

No Parking by Your Past Sins. Remember the prodigal son who entered a "no parking zone" and ended up in a pigpen. What a beautiful scene when he decided to remove himself from the muck and return to a productive way of life! God has promised to forgive and cleanse us if we just ask. Don't stay parked by your past sins.

No Parking by the "What Ifs" of Life. Many people are living in the "what ifs." A young girl with tears streaming down her face cries, "What if I had not had the abortion?" A young man staring out of a prison window says, "What if I hadn't pulled that trigger?" Some people know what it is to face an insurmountable barrier and refuse to park by it. One woman told of a husband who had one leg amputated in an accident, but she was thankful he still had one good leg left. This couple was not living by the *what if* area, but by the *what is* area.

I wonder how many of us are parked in the wrong zones? We blame ourselves for the old mistakes and old sins which God has long since removed from His memory. Are you letting the sorrow of *what ifs* rob you of the joy that is *what is?* Maybe we need to pray like this:

Lord, I have been in this parking zone too long. I have decided to move on and need your help. Forgive me for being overparked in the wrong zone. Let me come to you with clean hands and a pure heart. Help me live where there are no parking zones, and be free to serve you and experience joy in my life.

Stop to Enjoy the Fireworks

July is also Independence month, and I know many of you who do not live in Orange County, California, experience fireworks only once a year on July Fourth. But here, where I live, we get fireworks at least twice each night, all summer long. Disneyland in Anaheim has its fireworks show each night at nine, and Knott's Berry Farm in nearby Buena Park runs its fireworks show at 9:30 every night. If you're anywhere between those two fantasylands, you can see and hear two shows nightly! We had such fun at our last Spatula Ministries meeting, which meets right near Disneyland. Usually we have our own "fireworks" inside at our meeting, as devastated parents explode in pain and frustration at the firecrackers going off in their disintegrating family relationships. Last month, however, we paused during our Spatula meeting, and all of us went outside to enjoy the colorful display of fireworks going on just blocks away above Disneyland.

We all need to take time to enjoy the fireworks sometimes. Stop what you are doing long enough to enjoy the sunset, listen to a special song that lifts you up, or pick up the phone and share some special thought with a caring friend. I realized that night that we had heard the Disneyland fireworks display go on night after night for years. Usually it was an irritation to us, because it disturbed us from our intense sharing during out meetings. Sometimes we just paused and waited for the noise to stop so we could continue. See how much we were missing of the opportunity we had right here to pause and enjoy the brilliance of color and light? People all over the world would drive for miles to see what we considered an irritating interruption. How many times are you doing what we have been doing, letting something irritate you that could be turned into something really great?

> We must be frank and honest with God on what we have done wrong. Then we must relinquish it to God.

Be Guilt-Free

In the same way, our stay in Hurts Castle can be shortened if we can turn the bad experience of failure and sin into a good experience of restoration and forgiveness. We must be frank and honest with God on what we have done wrong; we must deal with it, accept our failure, and admit the wrong, admitting that we are *not* perfect. Then we must *relinquish* it to God, give to Him our failures, and reach out and accept God's cleansing and forgiveness. Then we can stand clean before the Lord! Many parents suffer needlessly because they have not dealt with their guilt and received the freedom to live guilt-free. This message of God's grace is captured perfectly by one of my favorite messages:

> Dear God, I have sinned against heaven and against you. I am no longer worthy to be called your child.
> My child, I know, I know. But my Son is forever worthy to be called your Savior.

God believes you are worth loving, even with your sins, even with that which is degrading to you, even with your faults, your shameful past, even your rebellion. If you were the only sinner in the whole world, God loves you so much that Jesus would have died for you alone!

Good news! Jesus was nailed to a cross so that you could stop nailing *yourself* to a cross. Accept *His* forgiveness and live a *guilt-free* life from here on out!

Binding Up the Wounded

The following article has helped me so much to articulate some of my feelings about guilt and Christian responsibility. I hope it will help you pass the time more profitably in "Hurts Castle."

Accepting Our Wounded

The other day I heard someone say, "The Christian army is the only army in the world that kills its wounded." . . .

Somehow that one phrase sums up the irony I see among God's kids. The very people who have the most potential to be kind and loving can also be the most cruel and judgmental. . . .

Choose any local church and you will find individuals that just don't fit into the mold. They go from church to church, looking for a place where they're accepted, or just stay on the fringes. . . . Certain behaviors that are unacceptable to the church group may even cause them to be "disfellowshipped." . . .

It seems that in our perfectionistic (and well-intentioned) desire to become more Godly, we often leave heaps of the less fortunate behind us—the ones that can't measure up to our ideals or overcome their problems. . . .

[Jesus'] life is like a poultice when applied to sick lives. . . . Sometimes I think part of the reason we ostracize failing Christians is that we're afraid somehow we'll be overcome with their problems and fail, too. . . .

134

We are all awed by . . . Mother Teresa on her hands and
knees with the dying and the orphans in India. But what
about the people on our own doorstep whose real need is
to be loved and accepted . . . ?

What will the body of Christ do with all of these opportunities? Will we ask them to go away until they are all
cleaned up? Will we be a hospital or a morgue?

MORGAN MCKENZIE

The challenge to act with God's grace and compassion
toward those who have hurt us so terribly, and especially
toward those who are less fortunate than we are, is clear.
Even when our child's actions stab our hearts with pain,
we need to remember that God loves him or her and His
acceptance is based on grace, not perfection. Here is a
short meditation that helps express the same idea.

I was hungry and you formed a humanities club
   And discussed my hunger. . . . Thank you.
      I was imprisoned and you crept off
Quietly to your chapel and prayed for my release.
   I was naked and in your mind you debated
      The morality of my appearance.
         I was sick and you knelt
      And thanked God for your health.
   I was homeless and you preached to me
      Of the shelter of the love of God.
   I was lonely and you left me alone
      To pray for me.
      You seem so holy; so close to God;
But I'm still very hungry, and lonely, and cold . . .

AUTHOR UNKNOWN

The few lines above may seem trite and oversimplistic,
but in actuality, love in action is the principle we are work-

ing with, and finding out that it does work. In order to act on our commitments, however, we must have spiritual nourishment. We must grow strong enough to put our thoughts and feelings into concrete steps which will make a difference—to us and to our hurting child. We need to keep the garbage out of our lives by feeding ourselves on the good, solid food of the Word of God, and by throwing out the junk food of our spiritual lives.

Garbage in the Salad

This story illustrates that principle. One day, as a mother was scraping and peeling the vegetables for a salad, her daughter came in to ask permission to go to a questionable non-Christian activity. On the defensive, the daughter admitted it was sensually stimulating, but the other girls were all going, and she wanted to go, since it wouldn't actually hurt her anyway, she argued.

As the girl talked, the mother quietly began to pick up handfuls of discarded vegetable scraps, mixing them in with the salad. When the daughter realized what she was doing, she cried out, "Mother! You are putting garbage in the salad!"

"Yes," her mother replied. "I know, but I thought if you don't mind putting garbage in your mind and heart, you certainly would not mind a little in your stomach!"

Thoughtfully, the girl removed the garbage from the salad, and with a brief "thank you" to her mother, she went out to tell her friends she would not be going with them.

If you are having trouble putting your love in action, maybe it's because you have allowed too much "garbage in the salad."

Checking Out of Hurts Castle

We don't have to stay in Hurts Castle forever. Healing does come eventually. Examine your feelings. Try to see in your life the process of healing that is taking place. Your emotions are more controlled now. Your tears may come, but not as often or as prolonged. You can actually "hold together" long enough to have a meaningful conversation with someone. Remember that this too shall pass. Someday you will look back at those first few months after your son or daughter devastated you, when you never thought you would live through it, and the sting will have gone. You will actually be able to enjoy your bittersweet memories. We recently spent ten days with our homosexual son, and had such an enjoyable time together. The painful times of the past are further away now, not constantly before me or over me like a black cloud. When I look at Larry, I see a beautiful young man, who has hurt and been hurt, and has grown through the experiences he had had. The same compassionate qualities he had before are still evident in his life. He is God's property, and it is God who will work in our lives, to perfect and continue that which he has begun.

Hang Tight!

Many have written us, asking how Larry is now. Our relationship with him has gone through enormous healing and restoration, which is what leaving Hurts Castle is all about anyway. But it wasn't easy, or quick. It has taken years, and we're not there yet. Someone told me to hang in, and hang out, and hang loose, and just don't decide to hang it all up! If you think about that, it might help you when you don't think you can hang on any longer. We are all in this together, and you are not alone. So hang on, hold together, look up, look inside, hang tight, and then after you have done all that, sit back and let God do the job. We are powerless to do anything except love our kids and pray for God's best for them.

Even when you are wallowing in your Hurts Castle, almost enjoying the bittersweet pain which is a part of healing, God can still remind you that His hand is on your life, even if you don't see it very often. Mercy is God not doing to us what we so richly deserve. Psalm 32:1 reminds us, "What happiness for those whose guilt has been forgiven! What joys when sins are covered over! What relief for those who have confessed their sins and God has cleared their record" (TLB).

When something happens in my life that just seems to crush me emotionally, or drain me spiritually, I take a self-imposed visit to Hurts Castle. I feel as though I'm all alone, with the weight of the world on my shoulders. I feel as if I just want my own little cocoon in the middle of the castle, where I can be alone for my own little pity party.

Although I did not need counseling after Bill's accident or even after Steven and Tim died, I sure needed help when Larry disappeared into the gay life. It was at the counseling center that I saw a young man who came in each week with a bag over his head. He couldn't bear for anyone even to see him! This poem is dedicated to that young man.

> I keep my bag right with me everywhere I go,
> In case I might need to wear it, so ME doesn't show.
> I'm so afraid to show you ME, afraid of what you'll do.
> You might laugh at ME, or say mean things . . .

Or I might lose you.
I'd like to take my bag off, to let you look at ME.
I want you to try to understand, and please, love what
you see.
So, if you'll be patient and close your eyes, I'll pull it off
so slow.
Please understand how much it hurts, to let the real
ME show.
Now my bag is taken off. I feel naked! Bare! So cold!
If you still love all that you see, you are my friend, pure
as gold.
I want to save my bag, and hold it in my hand.
I need to keep it handy in case someone doesn't
understand.
Please protect ME, my new friend, and thank you for
loving ME true.
But, please let me keep my bag with me until I love
ME, too.

AUTHOR UNKNOWN

Too often, those of us who have wayward children tend to throw "rocks" at our children for the hurt and disappointment they have caused us. Or, we throw rocks at others who, perhaps with good intentions, think they can analyze and solve our problems with two or three trite verses or sayings. I occasionally wished for a good-sized boulder to heave at some of my well-meaning friends who told me I shouldn't let my son's problems get me down.

Get a "First Stone"

Then someone gave me my very own stone to throw, but I haven't felt like throwing it yet. You see, this is a very special stone. Its story comes from the Bible. Jesus came upon some men who were preparing to stone a woman caught in adultery. Jesus questioned them as to their motives, and then challenged those assembled: "He that is without sin . . . cast the first stone" (see John 8:7 KJV). Jesus, the perfect Son of God, was the only one without sin. He could have thrown the first stone, but instead, He said to the woman, "Go and sin no more" (v. 11). My daughter-in-love, Shannon, has made me my own precious "First Stone."

As friends come in and ask me what the stone means, I reply, "Let me tell you a story. One day Jesus met a woman who was an adulteress. People all around were accusing her. Jesus said, 'The one of you who is without sin, let him cast the First Stone.' I keep this stone with my name on it to remind me that I cannot throw stones at anyone else." Then I go on to share how God's love can remove sin from us and bring us into wholeness through His Son. This is a simple illustration, yet it is so poignant and full of meaning for all of us.

When we are hurting, we need to realize that there are others who have been through the agony we are experiencing, and they can give us comfort and hope. Many parents have checked out of Hurts Castle, and they can encourage us like no others can. One of my favorite pastors, Chuck Swindoll, said recently that Christians can be like a sack of marbles: unfeeling, unloving, just clacking against each other as they go their way in life. Or Christians can be like a sack of grapes, able to comfort each other, pressing together to provide a soft, loving, warm place to cushion each other in the hard crushes of life. Let's all be like the soft grapes to others who are hurting and needing a comfort shelter, not like the hard, clacking marbles which are oblivious to those bleeding around them.

Depression Is Not Permanent

This poem about depression expresses so well what we sometimes feel like in our little castles of sorrow. There's nothing wrong with feeling depression—as long as we don't make it a permanent state of living.

DEPRESSION

Depression is a private thing
That even friends can't share—
No matter how they want to help,
No matter how they care.

Depression is a lonely thing
That beckons you apart—
Surrounded by a happy crowd,
Depression has our heart.

Depression is a human thing
That people cannot shun—
From beggars to majestic kings,
It comes to everyone.

Depression is a sometimes thing
That happens to us all—
But none can help like Jesus,
When depression comes to call.

AUTHOR UNKNOWN

We know that this did not come to stay, it came to pass. And your hurt will heal, your heart will start the mending process, life will go on, and *so will you!* You have started on a long journey to mending that tired heart, and we are with you on the trip. A friend said to me once, when I was hurting, "I'd like to wallpaper your hurting heart to mine." Sharing divides your sorrow, just as joy is multiplied by sharing. So reach out of your black pit, and we will provide you with a warm, loving hand to help pull each other along through this trip. Having someone who is going through the same feelings can help you make the passage without losing your grip on life. Put on the garment of praise for that spirit of heaviness, and it will help dispel the black clouds. Please read this article about healing, and let God minister his healing grace to your hurts.

We Don't Want to Be Healed

My husband and I have a wound which we do not necessarily want to have healed. That statement dismays many of our Christian friends who often remind us that God will heal it, *if we will let Him.* It just doesn't seem orthodox, somehow, for us not to want healing. But we have come to the conclusion that the only way the Lord can use us to reach others with such hurts is by keeping it open.

One of the heaviest burdens we had to bear when our son went home more than two years ago was the pious platitudes of well-meaning Christians who quoted Scripture, reminding us that God knows best; that He never makes a mistake, and that we are commanded to rejoice in all things. Rejoice that a part of our lives had been torn out? We wanted to scream, "What do you know about? You don't feel our hurt!"

We had studied the Bible for years; we had a head knowledge that God is adequate for our need. We knew that Peter, Paul, Stephen, and other biblical figures found

Him so. They lived nearly two thousand years ago; what did that have to do with us . . . today? We needed to have someone who had lived through such a tragedy tell us personally that this is so.

Among the cards and letters we received is one from a woman in Michigan who said, "I understand. I've been through it, and I feel your grief. God is adequate for your need." Here was someone who understood. Because she understood and cared enough to share our grief, a new ministry was opened to us in which we, in turn, help to share the sorrows of others.

Depending upon our availability, God has a special ministry for each of us—one which is uniquely suited to the individual—and He provides the means.

Part of my work as society editor for a local newspaper entails working with funeral directors and writing obituaries. By that means we are often directed to contact parents who have lost children—especially those who have, as we, watched a child waste away with cancer. Along with sharing their sorrow, we sometimes have opportunity to point them to the Lord Jesus Christ, the One who is completely adequate for their needs.

Contrary to what we are often told, time is not a great healer; it only dulls the pain. God alone can heal, but if there is any possibility that our healing will keep us from identifying with others who hurt, we do not want to be healed.

LOIS E. WORBOIS

July is our month for Hurts Castle, but please remember that your stay in Hurts Castle will not be permanent. You will recover, and God will use your hurt for something positive. Keep on hoping, and plan for the day you check out of Hurts Castle!

August

Coping between Estrogen and Death!

August is slowdown month for me. There aren't any holidays; most of our summer vacation company has come and gone, and out here in California, it's usually just too hot to do very much. Even inserting a new elastic band is work! I call August "go-to-pot" month. And aren't we all going to pot, either inch by inch or yard by yard? And it seems that when we are totally devastated by some catastrophe regarding our grown or almost-grown children, we go to pot mile by mile! Everybody in my camp is fighting one or two battles: the Battle of Fat and/or the Battle of Age. So August is dedicated to everyone who is battling alongside me for weight or age control. Remember, no matter how old or heavy you are, no matter how successful or not your diet is, your attitude makes the difference!

The Oil of Delay

Let's deal with the problem of aging, first. It's somewhat easier to deal with than weight, because there's not really much we can do about our age, short of lying on our driver's license!

One of the best ways I know to deal with and accept the marching of our age clock is with humor. (I know. I say humor solves almost everything; but it's true, and humor can help you face the fact that you, like every single other person who has ever lived, will keep growing older each day.) Here's a humor shot against premature aging!

I'M FINE

I'm fine, I'm fine.
There's nothing whatever the matter with me,
I'm just as healthy as I can be.
I have arthritis in both of my knees
And when I talk, I talk with a wheeze.
My pulse is weak and my blood is thin
But I'm awfully well for the shape I'm in.
My teeth eventually will have to come out
And I can't hear a word unless you shout.
I'm overweight and I can't get thin
But I'm awfully well for the shape I'm in.
Arch supports I have for my feet
Or I wouldn't be able to walk down the street.
Sleep is denied me every night
And every morning I'm really a sight.
My memory is bad and my head's a-spin
And I practically live on aspirin.
But I'm awfully well for the shape I'm in.
The moral is, as this tale unfolds,
That for you and me who are growing old,

145

It's better to say, "I'm fine," with a grin
Than to let people know the shape we're in!

Beginning at Forty

They say when you turn forty, life begins, but it begins to disintegrate! When you turn fifty, you really are in the stage between estrogen and death, and we are continually reminded that it takes more time and energy just to hold the line! So what if the aging process happens—it hits everyone! One good thing about aging is that *it isn't your fault!* How wonderful to know that this situation isn't caused by something we did or neglected to do! Inject some humor into your life! There are so many ways to do it. Let me share some ideas. Our lost youth is gone, gone, gone, but by letting ourselves become children again, we can tap into a boundless fountain within us, learning to laugh all over again. Kids laugh out of sheer joy: they don't need a good "reason." Quit taking yourself so seriously. Do some fun things, just because you want to be impulsive and adventurous. If your life is so planned out that you can't be flexible, then you have forgotten how to be like a child.

Hardening of the Attitudes

We know that "hardening of the attitudes" is a sure sign of advancing age, so hang loose in every area you can. Don't forget: Listen to that long-lost child you used to be, and catch the small, simple blessings, which are often so fleeting. Remember the sweetness of Indian summer; the sharp fragrance of orange peel, so reminiscent of Christmas; the surprise in children's eyes as they see the silvery sparkle of a frosty morning? Reflect on shared joys and rewarding friendships. Remember the sapphire sky and the sunset's afterglow? To see and appreciate these things all over again is like seeing the world through the eyes of a child. *Be a child again!* Let yourself recapture that childlike essence. We can be at peace with ourselves and forever young at heart as we *grow* through this stage together. We *know* age spots, wrinkles, and outward signs are showing, but so what? Keep that child alive and well inside you, and let the fall come. Look forward to September, which brings autumn, and reminds us we have crossed the bridge of lunch pails and milk money. Now we are *free* to enjoy each day and *be* a child instead of raising one. It is time to think of ways to inject fun into your life. It's wonderful to be childlike. Just don't confuse it with being childish! Here's an example:

Ego Strip

My 81-year-old mother is proud of the fact that she doesn't look her age. One summer day she went into a drugstore and, talking about the heat, said to the clerk, "Going to be ninety-seven today."

The man reached across the counter, shook her hand and said, "Happy birthday!" Mother took to her bed for a week.

ELANE TROQUILLE
SHREVEPORT (LA.) *TIMES*

I'd like you to think of aging as a marvelous adventure in uncharted lands, lands you will pass through only once—so enjoy them to the fullest. And always remember to keep a smile on your face and a chuckle on your lips. It's good therapy for aging. Try it on this fun piece, and see if laughing at aging helps you, too.

How to Tell You Are Growing Older

- Everything hurts and what doesn't hurt, doesn't work.
- You feel like the night before, and you haven't been anywhere.
- The gleam in your eye is from the sun hitting your bifocals.
- Your little, black book contains only names ending in M.D.
- You get winded playing chess.
- Your children begin to look middle-aged.
- You join a health club and don't go.
- Your mind makes contracts your body cannot meet.
- You know all the answers, but nobody asks you the questions.
- You look forward to a dull evening.
- You walk with your head held high, trying to get used to your bifocals.
- Your favorite part of the newspaper is "Twenty-five Years Ago Today."
- You turn out the lights for economic reasons instead of romantic ones.
- You sit in a rocking chair and can't get it going.
- Your knees buckle and your belt won't.
- You are seventeen around the neck, forty-two around the waist, and ninety around the golf course.

- You stop looking forward to your next birthday.
- Dialing long distance tires you out.
- You are startled the first time you are addressed as "old timer."
- You remember today that yesterday was your wedding anniversary.
- The best part of your day is over when your alarm clock goes off.
- You burn the midnight oil until after 9:00 P.M.
- Your back goes out more often than you do.
- The little gray-haired lady you help across the street is your wife.
- You get your exercise acting as pallbearer for friends who exercise.
- You have too much room in your house and not enough in the medicine cabinet.
- You sink your teeth into a steak, and they stay there.

Many of us have problems coping with aging and with death, which we will all face sooner or later. We tend to want to deny that we, or those we love, are growing older and growing closer each day to death. We think of death as a terrible ending instead of as the glorious beginning it really is. I don't think we should be morbid as Christians, plotting the time of our death with cold-blooded detachment, but I do think we should recognize that no one can escape from death forever. We should appreciate the life God has given us, and we should cultivate the riches of our loved ones around us from whom we may soon be separated.

Instant Aging

On a little lighter note, I want to share with you about a subject that can age all of us almost instantaneously: when our grown children move back home to live with us after some major catastrophe. While you are recovering from the shock of "second parenthood," enjoy the following humorous look at reparenting.

Thoughts to Console Parents Whose Kids Have Already Moved Back In

It's impossible to love the same child for twenty years. (After twenty years, it's not the same child.)

Grown-up kids are like winter storms. They may be late, but they never fail to show up.

Consider yourself a successful parent if they flip off the headlights before turning into the driveway at four in the morning.

Now that the kids are back, you don't have to eat leftovers. There aren't any.

Remember when you worried because you didn't know where your children were? Now, you do. They're back in their own rooms.

When children return to the family home, it's a gesture of reciprocal love. You drove them to school and now they're driving you up the wall.

Until they moved back home you never knew what cramped quarters meant.

You can't reason with them, and you can't hit them. How did they get so big and strong on junk food?

Why did they have to return just when everything started to click for you? (Your teeth, your knees, your back.)

It isn't aimed at you, personally. When newlyweds can't scratch up enough chicken feed to feather their own nest, they come home and pluck their parents.

You never realize what a happy marriage you've had until the kids move back—and then it's too late.

Before they left, the kids were deductible. Now, they're just taxing.

On Becoming Fifty

I will be fifty years old on my next birthday, and I never thought I would be so old while feeling so young.

I still clap when the hero or heroine comes to the rescue.

I still get totally engrossed in a game of Monopoly and feel like a self-made millionaire when I win.

I still think Christmas trees are always beautiful and never gaudy.

I still marvel at the colorful crocuses pushing through the snows of the disappearing winter.

I still think my favorite music can fill the corners of even the plainest room and make it beautiful.

I still come home from the public library loaded down with books and feeling very rich.

I still think learning new skills, no matter how minor, makes me that much more independent.

I still have faith in people, and am amazed when a few prove unworthy.

I still think a newborn kitten is a miracle to contemplate but never understand.

As I grow older, as everything must, I want very much to keep in touch always with the child within.

AUDREY JOHNSON

Dancing through Life

In addition to laughing, we need to step back from our own problems, get some perspective, and turn our liabilities into assets. Let's not wallow in our difficulties anymore; that doesn't help at all. Instead, let's look at our situation creatively, and see the humor and benefits of going through disaster!

If you can look at the inexorable march of time with humor, you can dance through life instead of marching. This popular little piece will help you start to dance through life with the humor it so aptly displays.

It's Much Later Than You Think

Everything is so much farther away than it used to be. It is twice as far to the corner, and they have added a hill, so I've noticed. I've given up running for the bus, as it leaves faster than it used to. It seems to me they are making stairs steeper than they used to in the old days. Have you noticed the smaller print they now use in the newspapers? There is no sense asking anyone to read aloud, everyone talks so low I can hardly hear them. And material in dresses is so skimpy now, especially around the waist and hips. It is almost impossible to reach my shoelaces. Even people are changing. They are so much younger than they used to be when I was their age. On the other hand, people my own age are so much older than I am. I ran into a classmate the other day, and she had aged so much she didn't even recognize me. I got to thinking about the poor thing while I was combing my hair this morning, and in doing so I glanced at my own reflection. Confound it, they don't make good mirrors like they used to!

Perspective is how we look at life, ourselves, and our problems. Some look at aging as a unique opportunity for fun. Those who grow older but insist on blaming it on a changing world react with a perspective, too. They deny their own participation in something one of us can avoid—aging—and refuse to take responsibility for their own human frailties. Most of us would give almost anything to be able to change reality, especially when our kids have sent us into a tailspin and we aren't sure we will survive (or even if we *want* to survive!). In such a situation, aging and weight problems tend to seem insurmountable. Just keep in mind that you are not alone; there are thousands of others in just the same kind of circumstances you find yourself. God will take care of you, just as He cares for others. We're all somewhere in that in-between age, fighting the battles of weight and senility. Remember, the Lord is right beside us, encouraging, admonishing, and setting goals for us. Give your best to God, and then forget about your pounds and years. No one is too heavy or too old to need and receive God's love.

Overweight or Undertall?

Now that we have found a good, constructive way to openly accept our aging as a great opportunity to try something new in God's plan for our lives, let's look at a problem most of us share along with aging: being overweight. This problem is not quite as easy to deal with. We have more responsibility in this area of our lives, and yet, being overweight is no excuse to check out of life and give up. Work at your weight the best you can, leave the rest up to the Lord, and learn to treat your weight problem with humor. It will help, and even though it doesn't burn very many calories to laugh, it does make dieting more enjoyable!

One of my friends, exasperated and frustrated after a particularly trying day, said to me, "Some days are just backward panty hose days! I don't know if I'm coming or going!" I also like this little idea of what our struggle with weight is like: Trying to keep your weight down is like going through life trying to hold a beach ball under water—it's just not possible!

Is the New Elastic Too Tight?

Don't give up on yourself if you are struggling with a diet. It is worth sticking to it, for your health and your self-confidence, to show that you *can* be in control of your life. But remember not to have *grim* determination, but *joyous* determination. Being able to laugh at your dieting struggles will take some of the pain away. How do you feel three days into a diet? Rotten? Miserable? As if your diet doesn't give you enough nutrition to support a small flea? Well, join the crowd and laugh with us.

I don't know who wrote it, but it so cleverly expresses the almost desperate attempts we sometimes make to justify our overweight and lack of self-control when we are on a diet. I'm not presenting it here to condone our blame placing, but because I know you will agree that those of us with weight problems sometimes feel like this. Yes, we do, even though we know we are ultimately responsible for the health of our bodies, no matter what our friends do or say. Enjoy the irony, but don't wallow in self-justification!

Dieting

Dieting is a social phenomenon. You wouldn't diet if you were living alone in the Gobi Desert. (No matter how fat you were, you'd still look pretty good compared to a camel.) Similarly, you probably wouldn't diet if all your friends bought their dresses from the racks marked "Chub-bette" or "Junior Plenty."

Unfortunately for you, however, your best friend has long, lean legs and a waistline the size of a napkin ring. If she gains ten pounds, nobody notices. If you gain ten pounds, your stomach keeps moving when you stop walking. And if you gain fifteen pounds, little kids sneak up behind you and make elephant noises.

So you diet. First you try counting calories of everything you eat. But this doesn't work because your calculator only has nine digits. Then you try those chocolate diet candies. But they taste so good you are reminded of the Hershey bars you hid in your panties drawer.

Next, you order some of those guaranteed diet pills from the "All You Can Eat Diet" advertised in *TV Guide*. After you have gorged yourself on cheesecake and Chee-tos, you read the guarantee's fine print which says the diet pill is "all you can eat."

In desperation you try a liquid protein diet. Finally, you have some success, but three weeks without food leads you to do strange things: like hyperventilating in a bakery shop to sniff up all the aroma; or leaving nose prints and drool on the window of the See's Candy Store.

Life would be much easier if you had only fat friends.

The Bottom Line

What is the bottom line on aging and dieting? The bottom line is that your future is in God's hands, not yours. You can spend thousands of dollars on age retarders and diet gimmicks, but ultimately, each of us is going to die and meet the Lord to account for our life situation. Then Jesus Christ won't be concerned about our age or our weight, but about whether we accepted His free gift of eternal life, which He purchased with His own blood on the cross. Looked at in that eternal perspective, aging and weight are not really as important as we sometimes think they are. So work through August in your calendar of recovery, and make some goals for yourself. Decide first to thank God for the blessings in your life, which are there *in spite of* your age and/or weight. Then inject some humor into your struggle with aging and weight. You'll find that you'll begin to look, act, and feel younger, and you will have one more area of your life where you can *cope.* You are growing, you are changing, you are maturing: you will win, with God's help!

September

Building Laughter in the Walls

On our calendar of recovery, September is our month for building and remembering the experiences our children will carry with them throughout their lives. It is a necessary part of growing up, and a necessary part of a parent's reflections on all of the precious yesterdays he or she shared with a child who is, perhaps, estranged and far away today. It is a true test of your new elastic! This story will illustrate what I mean.

The Red Jell-O Caper

One September evening, when my boys were young, I walked into the kitchen and found two of them sitting at the kitchen table, scooping up red raspberry Jell-O in a spoon and then flinging it against the white brick wall at the end of the table. They were laughing and having such sport watching the red Jell-O drip down the white brick, making irregular tracks on the wall. Such fun—until I came in!

157

Imagine my shock and how stunned I felt! How should I react? What should I say? I could have dumped the remaining Jell-O on their heads and sent them packing. I could have screamed and hollered and laid a heavy discipline trip on them. It was up to me to act responsibly. Here I was, making memories for life. This was a moment they would always remember. Would I react or would I go bananas?

The shimmering bowl of red Jell-O was only half gone. Evidently very little had been eaten, but the bulk of it was thrown nicely against the white bricks. What a shame to waste the other half dish of Jell-O, when I could be in on all the fun! They would have to clean it all up since they started it, but I would probably never have a better chance in my life to shoot Jell-O from the end of a spoon and watch it drip down the bricks, too!

So I sat down, put my purse on the floor beside me, picked up a *big tablespoon* (no sense fooling with teaspoons at this point), loaded up the spoon with a big glob of solid red stuff, and slung it carelessly against the wall. It was hilarious! I got another load on my spoon and let it fly. I could see why they had enjoyed this so much. Both of the boys decided I had made my decision to *enjoy* this, and they knew they would have to clean it all up, but now was time for fun.

So there we sat, all three of us, just slinging the red Jell-O as fast as we could, and laughing until we almost cried. They were laughing part out of fear and part shame, too, but we used up all the Jell-O and the wall was just a wet, dripping, red mess. The white brick didn't have a spot where the Jell-O had missed trickling down.

Did I handle this wrong? I guess my sense of humor helped me decide it would be more fun to join in the fun than to jump up and down and scream. Besides, these are memories that are being built into kids. They will never forget that day. And neither will I. Maybe that is what is meant by "building laughter in the walls."

Even though this house is silent now, and the boys are gone, and there is no red Jell-O dripping down the wall, our laughter still echoes from the walls. My boys have laughter safe in their own memories, too. Red Jell-O will *always* remind them of that day. I think my grandchildren will be told about the day that Barney threw all the Jell-O on the bricks (shooting it with a spoon), and how Grandma sat down and finished up the job with him.

Treasure the Good Memories

Are you building laughter in your home? Maybe not by throwing Jell-O, but by other avenues that make your home a happy memory place. Is it alive with music and singing and a clock that chimes, and some *life?* Living in a house can be so dull if you are not *alive* yourself. And laughter in the walls has to come from the people living in the home. Get some laughter into your life today, and then when the house is empty, you will remember all the laughter in the walls from the yesterdays full of laughter.

This poem says the same thing in a slightly different but equally valuable way.

THE HEART OF A CHILD

Whatever you write
On the heart of a child,

159

No water can wash it away.
The sands may be shifted
When billows are wild
And the efforts of time may decay.
Some stories may perish,
Some songs be forgot,
But this engraved record,
Time changes it not.
Whatever you write
In the heart of a child
A story of gladness or care—
That heaven has blessed
Or that earth has defiled,
Will linger unchangeably there.
Who writes it has sealed it
Forever and aye.
He must answer to God
On that great judgment day.

AUTHOR UNKNOWN

Memories are so important. Those of you who have a rebellious child probably are thinking right now that you don't want the memories, that thinking of happier times only makes the pain of today harder to bear. But, please, be grateful for what you and your child had before, and treasure it. It is too precious to waste. And use what you had before to help you bear what you have today.

Death is a separation even more real and permanent than that caused by sin in our children's lives. When I think of my son Steve, who lay dead for two days facedown in a rice paddy in Vietnam, I have to think of ways to wipe that horror away, like a windshield wiper erasing the memories that are traumatic. Then I must replace them with memories that bring me some happiness. By using this windshield-

160

wiper idea, it is possible to sift through many memories and pull out ones that are particularly meaningful.

Steve's Green Sweater

Like with Steve . . . I remember his sweater, a soft, wooly, light green color. His special girlfriend had made it for him when he was just about seventeen. He was so proud of it and it had been all hand-knit. It was the most special piece of clothing he had.

One day he spilled cocoa on it and was sure he had ruined it. He came in all upset and mad, but I quickly reassured him that I would wash it out and it would come out just fine. Immediately he protested: he knew I would shrink it or hurt it if I washed it.

The next day while he was at school, I decided to wash it for him. It came out just super! It looked brand-new. I folded it and put it away in his drawer.

That afternoon when I was shopping, I saw some Barbie and Ken doll clothes at the store. Imagine my delight when I saw a little puffy, green sweater, just exactly the color and style of Steve's sweater, but teeny tiny. I bought it, went home, and laid it out carefully on his bed.

Well, Steve came in from school, took one look at the tiny microsweater on his bed, and howled: "You ruined it! I just knew you would!" In a panic he tried to pull and stretch it, only to have it return to its original coaster size.

After he threw his anxiety fit, I calmly opened his dresser drawer, and there was his own precious green sweater, all clean and spotless, and just the right size.

The delight in his eyes was something I'll never forget. When I think of Steve today, I choose to think of that quick smile, and the twinkle in his eyes, as he lifted out that sweater and fingered the place where the stain had been. How much laughter was deposited in our walls that day!

This poem echoes the laughter we have in our walls. Are you building laughter in your walls?

THE VACANT SANDBOX

Vacant now, the sandbox stands.
No childish feet, no little hands
Sift the still and silent sands.

I close my eyes and I can see
Small children, in my memory,
Talking, laughing happily,
Building roads and bridges high,
Forts and castles to the sky.
But since, have many days gone by.

Those children, now to adults grown,
Have scattered far from childhood home
And they have children of their own.

Be patient, sandbox, for some day
When other children pass this way
You'll be a haven for their play.

CLARICE LANCASTER

Safe in His Palm

One of my most precious ceramics in my joy room is only about a foot high. The large hand of God, palm up, is cradling a tiny child, safe and secure in the Father's warm care. That is the image laughter in the walls reminds me of. And God's palm can be a place of rest for you, too, even if you are not a child, because God's loving care extends to us. When we cast our care upon Him, He cares for us. In the Bible God reminds us, "See, I have [carved] you on the palms of my hands" (Isa. 49:16 NIV).

A dear Christian woman, Robin Williams, composed this poem to remind us that in the process of building memories, we suffer some, too. It is up to God to pick us up, brush us off, kiss away our tears, and reassure us of His love, no matter what we have endured. So don't be afraid to look for the laughter in the walls, even though it carries with it the risk of being hurt.

RAG DOLL

Lord, I come to you like a broken rag doll,
My dress is torn and stained.
My arm is half-hanging on.
My eyes aren't shining and trusting like they once were.
And my expression isn't innocent and transparent
    anymore.

I'm not the unused, brand-new rag doll I once was.

Yes, my smile is still there,
But not as spontaneous as it once was;
It's a little more forced now;
A bit more tired.

I need to be picked up by you, Lord,
Picked up
   held tightly
    loved
     and reassured.

Reassured that no matter how I look,

Or how dirty and scuffed up and broken I am,
  You love me just like when I was brand-new.

Would you please hold me, Lord?

ROBIN WILLIAMS

If we want God to treat us like that, can we deny our wayward children the same treatment, both from God and from us? I know it hurts to love the child who has turned on you, whose actions pierce your heart sharper than any sword. But God's love is *unconditional*. Is yours? Think back to the memories you have in your walls. Think back to the good times you and your child had. Think back to the spiritual and emotional bond you two shared that is the unique bond of parent and child.

Leave the Results to God

Can you turn your back on your wayward child? Can you really forget the laughter in the walls? Don't turn away: face your child, forgive him or her, love him, and welcome him with open arms. You might even get hurt again, but you don't have to *agree* with your child, just to love him and reassure him of *your* love, which is as unconditional as that of God—no strings attached.

Yes, there is a risk to loving your child: you are vulnerable. You can get hurt. But the reward and the responsibility can give you a maturity, a close love, and a relationship nothing can ever replace.

God knows how much you are hurting because of what your child has said or done. And God knows that you are

164

not perfect, too. Leave the results up to God, and just trust him with your child.

Was It Worth It?

When I think of all the tragedy our family has endured over the years—Bill's accident, our two sons' deaths, our third son's estrangement, and the stress all of this put on my youngest son, Barney, the question immediately comes to mind: Was it worth it? Would I have been better off if I had never married, had never had children?

I don't even have to think about it: *No!* In spite of all the tragedy, and all the heartache, and all the sorrow, I wouldn't trade my life for any other life in the world. I have the laughter in the walls to remind me of the good times, and I have my God, who gives me the strength to survive the tragedy, and the joy to appreciate my blessings! Life without chance is not worth living, as this poem points out so well:

Tragedy

I always wanted a red balloon,
It only cost a dime,
But Ma said it was risky,
They broke so quickly,
And besides, she didn't have time;
And even if she did, she didn't
Think they were worth a dime.

We lived on a farm, and I only went
To one circus and fair,
And all the balloons I ever saw
Were there.

There were yellow ones and blue ones,
But the kind I liked the best
Were red, and I don't see why
She couldn't have stopped and said
That maybe I could have one—
But she didn't—I suppose that now
You can buy them anywheres,
And that they still sell red ones
At circuses and fairs.
I got a little money saved;
I got a lot of time,
I got no one to tell me how to spend my dime;
Plenty of balloons—but somehow
There's something died inside of me,
And I don't want one—now.

JILL SPARGUR

Please don't rob your children of their red balloons. Don't hush the laughter they're putting in the walls, because you want peace and quiet. Take the risk, let yourself go, love your child, and laugh with the laughter in the walls. No matter what suffering you go through later, the laughter you experience now will build you strong for those times of testing.

Wait with Open Arms

It's so much easier to fight for your child when he has gone astray if you can call on that strength developed through laughter. Then when your child turns her back, and heartache is your daily companion, you can join this unknown mother in her loving entreaty to her wayward child:

My Dear Prodigal Son:

Since you left home for the far country, your room in my heart is haunted with memories. One of those memories is of a time in the kitchen of our home. You were about two and a half years old. Although the issue that ignited the episode has been long forgotten, the war of our wills is as vivid as though it were yesterday.

In response to my instructions, you stretched your independence to a full two feet of toddler flesh, and defiantly refused to obey. Because your height did not intimidate me, you exerted the force of your young will against mine by throwing a "terrible twos" temper tantrum.

With maternal wisdom—or desperation—I sent you to your room with the command to "stay there until you are finished," finished meaning, "until you are ready to obey."

You trudged off with a stubborn swagger to your chubby walk. How long you stayed, I don't remember, but to a waiting mother, it seemed like a very long time.

What went on in your little mind and heart, I will never know, but finally I heard the door creak, and I watched as you came down the hall to the kitchen, ever so slowly. No longer was there any stubbornness in your walk, nor was there any swagger in your voice when you said, "I'se finished now, Mommy."

Now you are twenty-three years old, my son, and I am waiting in the kitchen of my heart, watching for the door of your resistance to God's love to open, listening for those words of surrender, "I'm finished now, Father."

With love and anticipation,
Mom

Can you wait with open arms for your prodigal son (or daughter) to come home? Can you love enough to risk again? Learning to forgive, to love with no strings attached, and to be willing to risk being hurt again, is an important step in your recovery. You've come a long way in the first three-quarters of your Year of Recovery. You've got the strength, the experience, and the determination to do it. Open up your heart right now, and expect that God is going to restore your child to you.

No, I don't mean that everything will be perfect, or that even the things that tore you two apart in the beginning will be healed. Not even fresh elastic can do that! But God will restore your love for each other, and he will be faithful to nurture your new love, a love which has weathered the storms of adversity and survived.

Give love a chance and make September your month to hear the laughter in the walls, a healing, soothing laughter that paves the way for restoration. It's worth it!

October
Whatever, Lord!

Happy October! Here it is autumn again, and the pungence of dry, fall leaves brings vivid recollections of the bittersweet days of autumns past. The smell of freshly cut grass reminds me of leisurely Sunday afternoons, when the still air was heavy with the combined perfume of assorted flowers and the grass on the wide expanse of the newly cut lawn. The scents of nostalgia . . . Hearing a long-forgotten melody can stir memories, and looking through a snapshot album always revives the past. Sometimes the association between a fragrance and something in the past is so ethereal that it cannot be recaptured, but will remain, hauntingly elusive. As we get older, and the gradual diminishing of the senses progresses, I hope for myself, that the sense of smell remains strong and functioning, so that I can recapture those bittersweet days in the past.

Adding Up the Victories

We've almost made it, you and I, in our year-long journey to recovery. When you look back at your life just a few short months ago, it's hard to believe, first, that things were that bad, and second, that you've come so far and still hurt so much now. Still, that new stretch of elastic *has* helped, hasn't it?

I know when I was slowly recovering from the devastation in our family when our son left us for a gay lifestyle, I thought each day was an eternity of suffering. I didn't think I'd ever have a day without a headache again, or an hour without tears. I was convinced that the rest of my life was going to be a blur of heartache, tears, and misery.

It took months of step-by-step recovery, just as we have been doing in our little symbolical "calendar," for me to finally believe that I would recover. It took even longer for me to believe, and then actually *see*, restoration with our son. We still have problems, and we still don't approve of his lifestyle, and there is still distance, but I can report some victories.

First, we *know* we love each other. We *know* that our love, based in the love of God, has withstood the test and is stronger than ever. No matter what happens, we love each other, no strings attached.

Second, I now know through my own experiences that misery does not have to be *permanent*. There is recovery. I do have days without headaches, nights without tears, weeks with joy and laughter. Life is worth living again, and I am stronger through what I went through.

Third, God has given me, and other recovering parents like me, the joy of being able to *share our recovery* with others who haven't been on the road as long as we have. I know our calendar of recovery works—it worked for me and it can work for you.

And then there are just so many valuable things God has given me and taught me through all of this. I have so many friends, so many people around the country who have been helped by my story, or who have helped me, or both. It is true that a life in Christ is a life rich in love and Christian companionship.

No, I wouldn't have chosen this life, but I wouldn't trade it for anything. My life is in God's hands, and I can't get much safer than that!

Why Me? versus Whatever, Lord!

Well, October is a tough month for us devastated parents. (You know by now that I don't mean the *real* month of October, but the "October," or tenth step in our twelve steps, or calendar, of recovery.) Why is October so tough? Because in October we learn *to accept God's will.* We learn to say, in the face of unbelievable chaos and tragedy, "Whatever, Lord!"

A life in Christ is a life rich in love and Christian companionship.

I heard this story about accepting one's life and it meant so much to me that I just have to share it with you all. There was a fellow who was on his way home in a subway. He was prone to motion sickness to begin with. He had eaten a big lunch and had worked all afternoon with an upset stomach. He was jammed into the subway as the last person on during rush hour. He was pressed against the glass of the door, facing everything flashing by him.

The longer he stood, the sicker he got, until the train stopped. It wasn't his stop, so he didn't get off, but the doors opened with a jolt. He couldn't hold it any longer. He threw up his whole lunch, and out it all came, all over the man standing closest on the platform. The door immediately slammed shut and the train moved on. The poor fellow standing on the platform was covered with another man's partially digested lunch. He turned to the man behind him and cried, "Why me?"

Nothing comes into the life of a Christian that God doesn't know about.

This is a perfect illustration of what it says in James; how we respond to trials by saying, "Why me? Why this? Why now?" We should instead say, "Okay, Lord: whatever!" In the first chapter, James says that trials are inevitable. If the door doesn't open on you this time, it will another time. So *be ready!*

We all have trials in our lives when we flail out at God and ask, "Why did you let this terrible thing happen to me?" And it is then that we should turn it around, and say, "Whatever, Lord!" We mean that whatever God sends into our lives has first passed through His filter. Nothing comes into the life of a Christian that God doesn't know about. Then you can just relax and kick it out of gear for a while and know that God will be with you during the trial. When "Whatever, Lord!" replaces "Why me?" then you know that you are on the way to growing through your trial or your crunch time. You are finally into the healing stage. You have survived the panic situation, and you are moving into normalcy again. Sometimes we wonder if there really is a normal state after the trauma we have come through. Robert Frost said he could sum up everything he had learned about life in three words: "It goes on!"

Isn't that really true? The human spirit can survive pain, loss, death, taxes, and life goes on, and on, and on. A friend wrote me today that we should live as if Christ died yesterday, arose this morning, and is coming back today! That helps us get some perspective on all the areas around us which seem like disaster zones. Your experience in the furnace will not last forever. In time, you will be able to look back and see how it all worked together for good in your life.

My encouraging word to all of you (again!) is that you develop a sense of humor to carry you through these days. Without a sense of humor you are doomed to despair, and yet with humor you can survive and actually enjoy the trip!

A Smiling Heart

This little poem will help you to begin saying, "Whatever, Lord!"

> If I can endure for this minute
> Whatever is happening to me,
> No matter how heavy my heart is
> Or how dark the moment may be—
> If I can but keep on believing
> What I know in my heart to be true,
> That darkness will fade with the morning
> And that this will pass away, too—

Then nothing in life can defeat me
For as long as this knowledge remains
I can suffer whatever is happening
For I know God will break all the chains
That are binding me tight in the darkness
And trying to fill me with fear—
For there is no night without dawning
And I know that my morning is near.

AUTHOR UNKNOWN

When you know that your morning is near, then you can rejoice in the dawn, and laugh with the sun. Do you ever have days when everything is so marvelous that you want just any small excuse to feel happy all over, like your heart is smiling? When I was in the depths of my suffering, I couldn't imagine ever feeling like that again, but it really is true that now I have days of a "smiling heart." It was worth the suffering to make it through to that again!

Abdicating Gracefully

It is said that as we grow older, we develop something called "hardening of the attitudes," and it does afflict parents particularly. As parents we have been on the top of the totem pole, the decision makers for so long, that it is difficult to learn how to abdicate gracefully, to allow our children to become adults.

We have to learn to train up a child and then let him go, but there is no magic button that turns a parent who has been the "omnipotent one" into just one opinion in his child's life.

Recently I read something about the wrongness of being right (it was given me just after one of my sons had told

174

me he felt that "I always had to be right"). The article was so good because it showed that being "right" shouldn't become a personal issue. We want to be right, and to fight back, if that's what it takes to be right.

For a Change: Listen

We pay quite a high bill for being someone who has to be right all the time. And why? Being right can be a losing proposition. If you are right all of the time, you will intimidate people and make it so hard for them to remember the facts, or even attempt to share them with you.

Are you as a parent one who has to have an opinion on everything and "share" it? If you are one of those parents afflicted with hardening of the attitudes and always know you are right, begin today to change things.

Decide you have no need to be right all of the time. Will your being right change the course of history? Second, resolve not to argue over things that have nothing to do with the situation at hand. Then try some active listening.

What is your son or daughter really saying? Then ask the Lord for wisdom. Wisdom is more important than knowledge. It is that innate "sense" which comes as a result of a regular communion with God, as well as from the wisdom in His Word, and our continuing to walk in the light He gives to us.

Finally, focus on the Lord's presence. Practice the presence of the Lord in your life. It's surprising sometimes how trivial our discussion may sound to the Maker of the Universe. This can be one big, giant step in the right direction toward restoration and recovery.

Part of learning "Whatever, Lord!" is learning that you don't have to be God to your kids all the time. In fact, most of the time, when relations are bad anyhow, you should just be quiet. Don't always be ready to jump in with judgment and instant divine analysis.

One mother gave me this advice: "Tell parents to stuff a fat sock into their mouths for at least six months." Doing this, of course, prevents them from saying all the wrong things, from admitting their ignorance, and mostly from destroying an already deteriorating relationship forever. So try it: Say, "Whatever, Lord!" regarding your rebellious child, and then stuff that sock into your mouth quick, before you become "Mrs. Know-it-all."

Let Go; Let God

The encouragement I can give you for October is to remember that God's grace and love are sufficient for *any* situation you could ever experience. God will listen to your fears, and assure you that He is in control. We all need daily cleansing. There is no pocket of sin which is too deep for God's love to restore us.

To parents with wayward children, our main thrust is that they pick up the pieces and go on with living. God can take a heart of stone and make it a heart of flesh, and God can bring conviction to those who walk away from Christian training.

Don't always look to complain to God about your life. Healing comes when we give God *all* the pieces. If you're having trouble accepting God's care for you in the midst of your problems, if you can't let go and let God, if you can't say a hearty, "Whatever, Lord!" then this letter is for you!

GOD'S LOVE LETTER TO YOU
(insert your name in blanks)

_____ , I love you! I shed my own blood for you to make you clean. You are clean now, so believe that it is true.

You are lovely in my eyes, and I created you to be just as you are. Do not criticize yourself or get down for not being perfect in your own eyes. This leads only to frustration. I want you to trust me—one step, one day at a time. Dwell in my power and in my love and be free! Be yourself! Don't allow other people to run you. I will guide you, if you let me. Be aware of my presence in everything. I give you patience, love, joy, peace, and life. Look to me for your answers. I am your Shepherd and will lead you. Follow me only! Do not ever forget this. Listen to me and I will tell you my will. I love you,

_____.

I love you! Let my love flow from you and spill over to all you touch. Do not be concerned with yourself—you are my responsibility. I will change you, and you will hardly know it is happening. You are to love yourself and love others simply because I love you. Take your eyes off yourself! Look only at me! I lead—I change—I create, but not when you are trying. I won't fight your efforts. You are mine. Let me give you joy, peace, and kindness. No one else can! Do you see, _____?

You belong to me. It is really none of your business how I deal with you. Do not struggle, but just relax in my love. My will is perfect! My love is sufficient! I will supply all of your needs according to my riches in glory. Look to me, _____. I love you! Trust me!

(Signed)
Your Heavenly Father

November

Letting the String Go

November is a month for snuggling in against the cold weather, looking back over the past months, and being thankful for what God has given us (sometimes we're thankful for what God *hasn't* given us). It's perfectly all right to look to the past constructively, to learn from it, and to appreciate where we've been. (Check the resiliency of your elastic.) But it isn't healthy to look back in regret and guilt. We have to be willing to "let go of the string" and let God take our balloons up in the sky, where they are in *His* power, not our own. This is the best material I have ever seen on what it really means to let go. Perhaps it is letting go of a rebellious child, or a burden of sorrow, losing a loved one, or learning to live with a heartache which we just cannot let go. Read this over. Study it, pray over it, and you will find that letting go of your load will release a peace within you. This will allow your spirit to soar, to be free, to be completely given to God. Let a work be done within *you*, which is where the need is anyway. Enjoy this. Share it. Keep this in your joy box for a down day.

LETTING GO

To let go doesn't mean to stop caring; it means I can't do it for someone else.

To let go is not to cut myself off, it's the realization that I can't control another.

To let go is not to enable, but to allow learning from natural consequences.

To let go is to admit powerlessness, which means the outcome is not in my hands.

To let go is not to try to change or blame another, I can only change myself.

To let go is not to care for, but to care about.

To let go is not to fix, but to be supportive.

To let go is not to judge, but to allow another to be a human being.

To let go is not to be in the middle arranging all the outcomes, but to allow others to affect their own outcomes.

To let go is not to be protective, it is to permit another to face reality.

To let go is not to deny but to accept.

To let go is not to nag, scold, or argue, but to search out my own shortcomings and to correct them.

To let go is not to adjust everything to my desires but to take each day as it comes and to cherish the moment.

To let go is not to criticize and regulate anyone but to try to become what I dream I can be.

To let go is not to regret the past but to grow and live for the future.

To let go is to fear less and love more.

A Life Lighter-Upper

My friend Mary Lou learned how to let go, and she is a shining example to me of the peace and joy God gives in the midst of grief, if we will only let go and give our burden to God. Some months ago she gave me a darling little music box with a yellow bird in it. It is unique because it works only when the sun hits the back of the music box. With the sunlight hitting it, it plays "You Light Up My Life." Such a special gift! Immediately I thought about God's love, which shines on us and brings a song and music to our lives. And it is the light of God which lights up *our* lives in this dark world. I enjoy my little bird so much that I sent one that plays "Amazing Grace" to a grieving friend in Texas, and what a scattering of joy that has been. Here is the letter she sent me after she received it:

> Dear Barb:
> What can I say, but thank you, thank you for my little singing bird. How darling, and the song "Amazing Grace" is special. It was played at our daughter's funeral, because that was one of her favorites. She was such a happy, full-of-life person, and she loved that hymn. So you see, my new, singing bird has far more meaning than you can believe! May the light of God shine on your ministry. The newsletters "light up my life" (another one of her favorites!), and I, in turn, am trying to help others who are hurting from many different causes.

I hope you can detect the gracious spirit this lady has. To some people, hearing that song would be a painful reminder of a tragedy, but to her, healing has come. She is able to think on Philippians 4:8: "Think on these things which are good, true, pure."

How refreshing to know that healing *does* come to us, and tragedies can become triumphs. Songs which could be full of pain and anguish can reflect God's perfect touch of comfort to our lives. Working with so many hurting parents, it is easy to see bitterness creep in and a sense of frustration and futility grow because of wayward kids, a suicide, or other family death. It is *then* that we have to depend on the love of God to warm our hearts, and give us that song. *Remember:* His love lights up our lives and brings music to our heavy hearts.

Letting Go Is Not Easy

Probably the very hardest thing you will have to do for your own recovery, and for the restoration of your relationship with your child, is to *let that child go!* Let him or her go and let God take over. It sounds so much easier than it really is, but it is essential to healing and restoration. Devastation in the family is not solved by a little Band-Aid. It takes major therapy and reconstructive surgery. Remember, children are not short-term notes, but long-term investments.

It is easier to let go if we are convinced that God cares about us, and that he considers us special enough to work things out to our very best advantage (even if it doesn't look much like it at first). I am reminded of how special our son and I are to God by a gift given me by another parent.

Us Somebodies

I received a beautiful, shiny red ceramic plate with white letters all around the rim spelling out YOU ARE SPECIAL TODAY. The custom was in early American families, that when someone deserved special praise or attention, they were served dinner on the red plate. This is a great way to give honor to a special person for some visible reminder of love. It reminds me that I am special today to God, even if it isn't my birthday, or Mother's Day, or any other holiday. God loves me every day, and I am always special to Him.

I am off the heavy guilt trip, because Jesus has wiped the slate clean. He cannot see my sin because it is covered by His blood. Remember, He gave me a white robe of righteousness which is kept clean by a special detergent called *forgiveness*.

It is not due to my own merit, but to "Christ in me, the hope of glory," that I deserve this special plate every day of my life. It reminds me how special I am to God; how He would have died for me even if I had been the only one in the world. I am *somebody* in God's sight, and *so are you!*

Gift Wrapped for God

So, confident in God's love and acceptance, let go and let God take your child. Give him to God! "But *how* can I give my child to God?" parents ask me over and over. I go through my routine about "nailing them to the cross," "zipping them up, putting them in his care," and so forth. But sometimes parents are in such emotional turmoil that they hear the words, but they need some real thought pattern to help them understand what I mean. Recently I heard this illustration which really helps.

Picture in your mind that you are placing your daughter or son into a gift box. Then wrap the box with lovely paper and a ribbon. Next, imagine the glorious throne of God, which is at the top of a long flight of stairs. Mentally walk up those stairs, carrying your lovely, wrapped package. Put it down at the feet of Jesus, who sits on the throne. Wait there as He bends down and picks up the package, putting it on His lap. He removes the wrappings, takes off the lid of the box, and then lifts our child out. Jesus wraps the child in His loving arms and holds him close.

After you have seen Jesus holding him, you then walk back down the stairs, pausing partway down to check back, to reassure yourself that Jesus still has your child in His arms. Then you continue down the stairs, thanking God for taking control.

That Settles It!

You have given your prodigal to God and have taken your hands off. Now you are ready to ask God to do whatever is necessary to bring that child back to Him. We may see circumstances that tear us apart, but God will undertake to reach the rebel, often in very dramatic ways. Whenever you are tempted to take control again, you must practice this little thought exercise and remember the definite time when you presented your child as a gift to the Lord, and He received him in faithful love.

The only time you have permission to take your child back is when Jesus drops him! When do you think that will be? Never! Then don't worry—Jesus has him in His arms, and you can't do nearly as well with your child as Jesus can.

If your prodigal is not home, and you have truly done this little thought exercise, then you know you cannot let the sin of one family member disrupt and destroy the entire family. So get on with it! There is work to be done! Leave your child with the Lord! To pick up your child is about as useful as rearranging furniture on the *Titanic* rather than getting on with life!

Sometimes I think the parents who write me are more of an inspiration to me than I am to them! This letter is from a mother who first wrote me when she was in complete devastation. She has a toddler as well as a physically handicapped child. Her mother is a lesbian and her father is dying of cancer, but now she is praising God because He is in control. She has truly let go of the strings for each of her loved ones, knowing that God can take better care of them than she can. This is her letter:

Dear Barb:

The past year or so has been difficult. Matt is still lying on the floor, blind and mute, and practically immobile. My mother has decided that reincarnation is the truth (funny, the sin of homosexuality never really bothered me because it's "just a sin," but to turn your back on Jesus . . . whew!). And our business is just afloat and my father is dying of liver cancer, and I haven't had an hour alone with my husband for five and one-half years and . . .

But you know what? I've read the back of the book, and we win! I suppose what I have is either the peace that Jesus gives, or I've fallen off the edge! Either way, it's super to know God is in control!

I know this woman: she's not pretending. All those things are true about her family members, and she really is praising God because He is in control! She is such an example of a thankful heart.

The Trusting, Sharing Heart

The person who is unable to let the string go is the person who does not trust God. It doesn't have to do with whim; it has to do with *trust*. If we really trust God, then we won't fear anything. If we really trust God, then we can meet the challenges of life head-on, knowing that in the end, God's side "wins."

The trusting heart is the sharing heart. The trusting heart can look outside of its own predicament, see the plight of others, and offer help. The trusting heart is just waiting to be used by God for His master plan. What a contrast there is between the trusting heart and the self-centered, self-pitying heart described below.

As I serve the turkey, fresh fruit, and vegetables and pies to my family, don't tell me . . . about those in China who only have a cup of rice to eat each day of their lives . . . or those who lie on garbage that others throw away . . . or those in Africa who have to resort to eating insects to keep from starving.

As I wash, sort, and put away the permanent press, double knit, mix 'n' match wardrobe of my family, don't tell me . . . about those who have to weave their own clothes by hand . . . or those who only have the clothes on their backs.

As I dust our fine furniture, vacuum our plush carpeting, and wash our sparkling china and crystal, don't tell me . . . about those who live every day in the streets . . . who have no shelter . . . and whose possessions are only what they can carry.

As I regulate the heat from the furnace or the cool air from the central air conditioner, don't tell me . . . about those who live without heat in subzero weather because they cannot pay their utility bills . . . or about those who live amidst intense heat without benefit of even a cooling breeze.

As I sit on the patio with a cold beverage and a good book, enjoying the afternoon sun, don't tell me . . . about the woman in Haiti who spends twelve hours each day pounding boulders into pebbles to earn a dollar each week.

As I draw fresh, clear water from the faucet, don't tell me . . . about those in Thailand and India who use the water from the river, stagnant with debris, human waste, and dead bodies.

As I slide under the clean sheets and soft blanket of my bed at night, don't tell me . . . about those in Hong Kong, India, or Bangladesh who sleep in cold gutters or in the dirty streets.

As I sit in the comfortable, padded pew, glance at the beautiful stained-glass windows, listen to the strains of a familiar hymn, and hear the Word of God explained, don't tell me . . . of those who know not Jesus . . . or those who maim themselves to serve their spirits . . . or those who prostrate themselves before a lifeless stone god.

Don't tell me . . . I am afraid to know.

Don't tell me . . . I am too comfortable.

Don't tell me . . . I might begin to care.

AUTHOR UNKNOWN

Doesn't that tell us something about our own concerns for our children? Are we closing our eyes to reality concerning our wayward children because we are afraid to know, too comfortable to make hard decisions, and too afraid our caring will make us vulnerable to more hurt?

And yet, it is our knowing, our uneasiness, and our caring that should compel us as parents to bring our rebellious children to the Lord, to lay them at His feet, and then to let Him take action on their behalf. Let's start practicing that today. Let November be your month to care enough about your child to let him or her *go!*

One of the surest evidences of faith in God is our being able to turn away from a difficult situation in which we have done our best, and to give our attention to other matters with a calm, untroubled mind. Let go—and let God!

Carrying on our theme of caring enough to take action, let me share the following poem with you. See what a difference caring can make!

A Friend Like You

Everyone needs a friend like you.

You found me lying on your doorstep
with broken wings, covered with dirt.
   Like a torn up piece of cloth
   Like a battered old toy
   Like a gaping, ugly sore
   That hurts even to look at
     Or touch
     Or care about.
Alone
Afraid
Injured

And yet you opened the door and gently let me in.

You bandaged the wounds
And soothed the raw edges where it hurt the most
You set my broken bones in place
And pieced back together my shattered dreams.

What I thought was the end
Was really
The beginning.

You invited me on a journey . . .

> to pioneer an unexplored territory
> to blaze a new trail
> to open new doors
> to see a new horizon

Oh, yes, I want to go!

The warmth in your smile
And the care in your eye told me I was safe.

But . . . I tire so easily
   And I'm really not very brave
   And I'm not sure just exactly where it is I'm going
Or just what I'll find once I get there.

Then I took one step . . .
As if to believe you really are there.
. . . and then I see you mean what you say.
You *do* care.

You held my hand across the rough places
And gave me a boost over the high fences
You let me run free across the fields

Always there
Always with me
Even if I ran ahead
Or tagged behind
Always gently pursuing me to go on

Yet totally accepting me right where I was . . .
   on the rocks
   on the fence
   in the mud
   up a tree
   in the field

Along the way you teach me things . . .
   how to swim—so I won't be afraid of the water
   how to fish—so I can feed myself
   how to land—so I won't be afraid to fly
   how to cry—so I won't be afraid to hurt
   how to get up—so I won't be afraid to fall
   how to love—so I won't be afraid to give.

My injuries are healing
My soul is awakening
My eyes are not afraid to look at
   where I've been
   where I am
   where I'm going

Even though I'm unsure of where I am now
I've never been here before
And even though it's exciting and new
It still scares me
It's all so different than what I'm used to . . .
   unfamiliar feelings
   and sights and sounds and smells

But I'll walk on with you.
I trust your outstretched arms and your faithful carings.

Thank you for mending my broken heart
For soothing my aches
   hearing my cries
     understanding my pain
      sharing my grief.

How [blest] I am!

Everyone needs a friend like you!

SARAH STERLING

Two Important Steps

So November's step to recovery is twofold: *let go* and *care*. With a combination like that, you will only succeed. Recovery is on the way. Wholeness is around the corner. Life is once again worth living.

Did you ever think of your life, with all the mistakes, sins, and woes of the past, like tangles in a yarn ball, with such a mess that you could never begin to straighten it out?

It is such a comfort to drop the tangles of life into God's hands—and then leave them there. If there is only one message I could get through to you this month, it would be to help you place your child in God's hands, and then release the load to him. God alone can untangle the threads of our lives.

What a joy and comfort it can be for us to drop all the tangles of life into God's hands, and then to leave them there!

December

No Microwave Maturity

When I get all the way to December, I feel as if I have really accomplished a lot. Just surviving is a big achievement! (Did you find that all those snippets of varying sizes of elastic helped you s-t-r-e-t-c-h to your full potential?) Sometimes, however, when I dwell on the problems in *my* life, I get frustrated with what I am often tempted to see as lack of progress on God's part. Why aren't I more mature? Why do little things still bother me? Remember the old saying, "I want patience, God, and I want it *now*"? Well, there is no such thing as *microwave maturity*. We get maturity the hard way—we *earn* it.

Idle Your Motor

I think the most comfort to people who have to be patient in their situation is this: "Patience is the ability to idle your motor when you feel like stripping your gears!" So many letters come to us reflecting parents' inability to be patient and wait for God to touch their children's lives and hearts. God has to touch that core inside and cause change to come in His own timing. There is a reversal process which takes time, and we are all learning about patience. One helpful prayer called "reversal" goes like this: "Lord, for so long I thought Your love demanded that I change. At last, I am beginning to understand that Your love changed *me!*"

God loves me so much that He will accept me just as I am, but He loves me too much to leave me that way!

Saints and Sinners

When some fellow yields to temptation
And breaks a conventional law,
We look for no good in his makeup,
Oh, Lord, how we look for the flaw!
No one asks, "Who did the tempting?"
Nor allows for the battles he's fought.
His name becomes food for the jackals,
The saints who have never been caught.
I'm a sinner, Oh, Lord, and I know it.
I am weak, and I blunder and fail.
I am tossed on life's stormy ocean
Like a ship that is caught in a gale.
I am willing to trust in Thy mercy,
To keep the commandments You taught.
But deliver me, Lord, from the judgment
Of the saints who have never been caught.

By now you have traveled through eleven whole steps of recovery. You are on the mend. Your family is on the mend. Your relationship with your child is on the mend. "Impossible!" you say, "I haven't even seen my child. I don't know where he is, or what he's doing!" (Yes, but you have seen God working in your own life, and you know what *you* are doing! Restoration can come a long way, even before you ever see your rebellious child, so take heart!)

How Dry I Am!

Look back over the last few months of your life. Can you see the progress you have made? I remember when I was overjoyed the first time I went one whole day without crying! Have you had a "dry" day yet? Congratulate yourself on your progress, no matter how slight it might be. You are working on it and trusting God, and that's all that counts.

Often when we start to recover, we slump back into a depression. That's because we get a little taste of wholeness, and then we don't have the patience to wait for the rest of the situation to be resolved.

Don't fall into the depression trap when you have been doing so well. Carefully study the following four steps out of depression, and decide right now that you won't slip back, but you will go forward!

Four Steps out of Depression

1. Realize you are depressed.
2. Tell yourself this is not a *permanent* thing. It is passing.
3. Anything that is going to leave can be endured for a short time.
4. Set a deadline for it to end, and tell yourself you will allow your depression to last until a certain time—and then you will be rid of it.

You yourself can decide if you will be happy or sad, and you can be in control of your moods much of the time by using this simple system. Give it a whirl!

This week I had a really special blessing. I heard someone twist up a verse which brought a new facet of its meaning to me. The verse is Proverbs 13:12: "Hope deferred makes the heart sick; but when dreams come true at last, there is life and joy" (TLB). I heard a new Christian, who had heard the verse and was trying to pass it on to a friend who needed comfort, say, "It's so good to have hope. It's the *waiting* that spoils it!"

Goldbricking

For Christmas (whether you are reading this at Christmastime or not doesn't matter—have Christmas in July, if that's when you're reading this), I have a great idea that is sort of like "occupational therapy." If you do it, I can guarantee that you will lift out of your slump and be able to work on learning patience. This idea doesn't even cost very much.

Do this first of all, for yourself, and then reach out to someone else. First, get yourself a used brick. Find one around or buy one for under twenty cents at a builder's supply place.

Then find some bright, shiny *gold*-colored wrapping paper and wrap this brick up carefully. Place a colorful bow around it, and perhaps some berries or a sprig of Christmas color.

Now you have a beautiful gold brick to use as a doorstopper! But mostly, this is to remind you that *you are gold in the making!* The furnace of pain you are going through is making you gold for the Master's use. You are being refined, purified, tried, and made worthy.

Did you know that if all of the gold in the whole world were melted down into a solid cube it would be about the size of an eight-room house? If you had all of that gold, billions of dollars worth, you could not buy a friend, character, peace of mind, a clear conscience, or eternal life! And yet, you are gold in the making because of the trials you have come through! Isn't that an exciting idea!

Now, after you have your shiny, gold-wrapped brick nicely sitting by your door as a stopper, you get another one. Wrap it in the same kind of paper, add a sprig of holly, and select a good friend, perhaps someone who has been a "gold brick" in your life—one who has refreshed and encouraged you, and who might need some lifting in her own life right now. Take your second gold brick to her, and tell that person how she has blessed you, how you have wanted to remind her how she has helped you through your time of testing.

Before long, you will be making your gold bricks by the dozen, and spreading this idea to others. All the time, you will be refreshing them, and at that same time making yourself aware of your many friends who are like gold in your own life!

If I come to visit you, I hope I'll see your gold brick by your front door—a constant reminder to you and to others of how we are all gold in the making!

While we are in December of your Year of Recovery, perhaps you can relate to this funny, funny mother!

SEE MOTHER, FUNNY, FUNNY MOTHER

See Mother. See Mother laugh, Mother is happy.
Mother is happy about Christmas.
Mother has many plans. Mother has many plans for
    Christmas.
Mother is organized. Mother smiles all the time.
Funny, funny Mother.
See Mother. See Mother smile. Mother is happy.
The shopping is all done. See the children watch TV.
    Watch children, watch.
See the children change their minds.
See them ask Santa for different toys.
Look. Look. Mother is not smiling. Funny, funny
    mother.

See Mother. See Mother sew.
Mother will make dresses. Mother will make robes.
    Mother will make skirts.
See Mother put the zipper in wrong.
See Mother sew the dress on the wrong side.
See Mother cut the skirt too short.
See Mother put the materials away until January.
Look. Look. See Mother take a tranquilizer.
Funny, funny Mother.

See Mother. See Mother buy raisins and nuts.
See Mother buy candied pineapple and powdered sugar
See Mother buy flour, and dates, and pecans, and
    brown sugar, and bananas, and spices, and vanilla.
Look. Look. Mother is mixing everything together.
See the children press out cookies.
See the flour on their elbows.
See the cookies burn. See the cake fall.
See the children pull taffy. See Mother pull her hair.

See Mother clean the kitchen with the garden hose.
Funny, funny Mother.

See Mother. See Mother wrap presents. See Mother
  look for the end on the Scotch tape roll. See Mother
  bite her fingernails.
See Mother go. See Mother go to the store ten times in
  one hour. Go, Mother, go.
See Mother go faster. Run, Mother, run.
See Mother trim the tree. See Mother have a party. See
  Mother make popcorn. See Mother wash the walls.
  See Mother scrub the rug.
See Mother tear up organized plan.
See Mother forget gift for Uncle Harold. See Mother get
  hives.
Go, Mother, go. See the faraway look in Mother's eyes.
Mother has become disorganized. Mother has become
  disoriented.
Funny, funny Mother.

It is finally Christmas morning. See the happy family.
See Father smile. Father is happy. Smile, Father, smile.
Father loves fruitcake. Father loves Christmas pudding.
Father loves all his new neckties.
Look. Look. See the happy children. See the children's
  toys.
Santa was very good to the children. The children will
  remember this Christmas.

See Mother. Mother is slumped in a chair. Mother is
  crying uncontrollably.
Mother does not look well. Mother has ugly dark circles
  under her bloodshot eyes.
Everyone helps Mother to her bed. See Mother sleep
  quietly under heavy sedation. See Mother smile.
  Funny, funny Mother.

You Are Not Alone

I could share literally dozens of letters with you from people who are making progress on their journey to becoming whole people again. *You are not alone.* Take my word for it, your black-pit days will pass, and balance will return to your life.

Those of us who have rebellious prodigals can rejoice with each other at our successes, and cry with each other when things go wrong. We are bound together because of the special grief we have had, and our common suffering is a far greater link than common joy. However, for this month let's concentrate on the inner joy we can have, and set our grief aside for a little while. We are growing, maturing, and learning to live in the real world again.

You are not alone. There are thousands of us who have felt as you do now, who hurt as you are hurting, and we are making it. We are survivors, and you will be too. Just find comfort in knowing that you are not by yourself. Your maturity will come—be patient!

Even with our battered egos and psyches and other bruises and bumps, we are still valuable to God as gold in the making. The following is a good illustration of what I mean.

You Are Deliverable!

A package was delivered to me, and on it was marked DAMAGED IN TRANSIT, BUT DELIVERABLE. There was a space at the top that said either DELIVERABLE or UNDELIVERABLE, and a big black crayon marked this package as DELIVERABLE! The string was hanging off it, the label was torn off, and tapes were hanging out of one corner, but it was still deliverable.

I thought of how many lives like mine are damaged and hurt. We should be marked FRAGILE: HANDLE WITH CARE, but we are like packages on a long and bumpy journey toward maturity. We have been crushed with the pain of losing a child, or the heartache of a child abandoning us, or rebelling against us and God, but instead of being handled like fine china, we are slammed from one side to another. On that long journey we are DAMAGED IN TRANSIT, we have been unraveled, unglued, undone, and are coming apart at all the corners.

Damaged in Transit, but Deliverable. That's us.

We have been shoved against the walls of despair and frustration; handled carelessly with no thought for the fragile heart inside, which is already bleeding and broken—and we certainly don't need any more crushing.

But you know, even though we may be damaged in transit, we are still DELIVERABLE! We are on that long trip. DESTINATION: The Heavenly City, the New Jerusalem, where we will rejoice around the throne of God. The Master will claim me and fix me all up. I will withstand the shocks of life and God will claim His package. My label may be torn off, but my destination is clearly marked GLORY.

Learn how to lay down your agonies, pick up your credentials, and continue on. There is no instant glory. It is a long trip for most of us, but we can help each other on the journey by loving, caring, sharing, and softening the blows of life. DAMAGED IN TRANSIT, *but* DELIVERABLE. That's us. Hang in there with us. You are not isolated. We are on the same trip. Some are farther along, and some are behind you, but we are all on the same road. Let's arrive and be claimed by the Lord as part of His family. We'll have plenty of time to get really close in heaven. There is no unclaimed freight in God's family!

Heavenly Eraser

Not only do we have to learn patience for our own maturity, we also have to learn to be patient with our children. Because of the fast days in which we live, we are used to fast foods, rapid transit, microwave ovens, and instant breakfasts. But instant emotional maturity? There ain't no such thing!

Maturity is a process. There are no instant results. But over the long haul, you can see a softening, a smoothing out of the rough edges, a sensitivity to God's working in their lives, a lessening of the pain they have experienced and even inflicted on themselves and on you.

Habits are first cobwebs, and then cables. You cannot toss a habit out the window. It must be coaxed down the stairs one step at a time. God turns the spotlight of His cleansing Spirit on all the dark corners of our hearts, and our minds, and our spirits. All of the *yuk* has to be removed.

Someone once told me that God has a gentle heavenly eraser. It erases slowly sometimes, but it leaves no traces, and it doesn't tear the paper. That's better than a quick, fast swipe that tears as it erases. Remember: You who have endured the stinging experiences are the choicest counselors God can use.

It's Time to Go Shopping

As we move closer to that spiritual maturity which will be ours when we get to heaven, we should remember what that maturity is made out of. Let's not just wait passively for God to sprinkle magic dust on us that will transform us without any participation on our part. Let's go "shopping" for the best ingredients to slow and steady maturity.

Shopping List

It's time to go shopping again.

All of a sudden I've noticed that I'm completely out of generosity—I must look for some more.

I also want to exchange the self-satisfaction I picked up the other day for some real humility. I've heard it wears better.

And I mustn't forget to look for some tolerance, it's a good substitute when you're low on indulgence, and the last time I was shopping I saw some interesting samples of kindness I want to look at again.

Oh, I almost forgot—I must try to match some patience, too. I saw some on a friend yesterday, and it was very becoming.

Come to think of it, I must also remember to get my sense of humor mended, and keep my eyes open for some goodness—it's surprising how quickly one's stock of goodness becomes depleted.

Since there are several items on my list, I might as well make a day of it and indulge in a real shopping spree.

It would be a good idea for me to check to see if there is a special being offered on charity, optimism, and love—things a person should never risk running out of.

Yes, it's time to go shopping again. With such a long list, I'm sure glad the store is open all hours of the day and night, and that the Shopkeeper is so understanding.

Otherwise, my negligence in letting these supplies run down so low could cost me dearly. As it is, the only price I'll have to pay will be faith.

Yes, God, it's time to go shopping again.

So when you go forth to recover after your year of molding, know that your maturity will keep increasing every day of your life, even when you don't feel that God is doing anything with you. Here is a great illustration of God's secret maturing work. Keep this where you can see it often, and be reminded that God cares even when you don't see Him working.

Waking Up at Home

A little child is so busy playing that he hardly knows he's growing tired. Suddenly sleep overtakes him right where he is. His mother finds him curled up on the hard floor, thumb in mouth, cheek pillowed on a toy. When he wakes up he's in his jammies, in his own room, in his own bed, yet he never remembers being picked up, carried, undressed, and tucked in.

Sometimes we get so busy with our busy-ness, so wrapped up in ourselves, that we fall asleep spiritually. For days, or months, or years we do not think about God, talk to Him, or listen for His voice. When we wake up needing Him and seek Him out, we find He's there. How glad we are to feel His presence!

In our newfound joy we mourn the time we were asleep, feeling it was a wasted, lost time. But we forget that God wasn't ignoring us while we were ignorant of Him. He carried us in His thoughts even when we thought we had left Him behind. In some mysterious way God found us, rescued us, changed us, and brought us home even before we awoke to His presence. This is the miracle of our Lord's dependable love. No matter what far country we go to, no matter how lost we become, we can wake up to find ourselves at home with Him.

MARGARET PARKER

The Master Potter

As we wind down our year's journey, I want to remind you again that God is in charge. From a seemingly useless lump of clay, He can fashion something beautiful and useful, as this story so vividly points out:

The Beautiful Teacup

A couple in England passed a china shop, which had a lovely teacup displayed in the window. They went inside to see it more closely, but suddenly the teacup spoke!

"You don't understand. I haven't always been a teacup. There was a time when I was a lump of red clay. My master took me and rolled me and patted me over and over. I screamed for him to stop, to leave me alone. But he continued to mold me, answering, 'Not yet.'

"Then I was placed on a wheel and spun around and around. It made me dizzy, spinning on and on like that. But he didn't stop when I was begging him to take me off the wheel. He continued shaping and molding, and then put me in an oven!

"I have never felt such intense heat! I wondered if he wanted me to burn up. And I screamed and beat on the door to get out. I could see the master through the opening. And I read his lips as he said, 'Not yet.'

"Finally, the door did open. He put me up on a shelf and I began to cool. That felt better. Then suddenly, he brushed me, and painted me all over. The fumes were terrible! I thought I would surely choke to death. I was gasping for air and hurting inside from the heat and choking fumes.

"Soon he put me into anther oven. It wasn't the first one, but it was twice as hot! I knew for sure that this time

I would suffocate. I begged my master to stop. All the time I could see him shaking his head and saying, 'Not yet.'

"I felt there was no help. I knew I could never make it. I was ready to give up. But just then the door opened. He took me out, and I could see that he was pleased with his work. He handed me a mirror and told me to look at myself. I did. And I said, 'That's not *me!* It couldn't be! I am so shiny and beautiful!'

"Then he said to me, 'I want you to know that I had to roll and pat you to shape you. If I had left you, then you would have dried up. And I know the wheel made you dizzy and sick, but if I had stopped, you would have crumbled. I know it hurt and was hot and disagreeable in the baking oven, but if I hadn't put you there, you would have cracked. I know the fumes were bad, when I brushed you and then painted you all over, but you see, if I hadn't done that, you would never have hardened. And if I had not put you in the second oven, you would not have survived for very long, you would have been brittle.'

"'Now you are a finished product. You are what I had in mind when I first began with you as a lump of clay!'"

Pulling It All Together

Remember, you cannot give the final score on a life until the game is over, and it isn't over yet with your child. Remind yourself daily that God called on you only to be faithful; he didn't call you to be successful.

These words, written by a dear friend, say it all:

He didn't bring you this far to leave you.
He didn't teach you to swim to let you drown.
He didn't build His home in you to move away.
He didn't lift you up to let you down.

God's mill grinds slowly but exceedingly fine. His refining fire is hot, and nothing can come into your life except through the filter of God's love. So go on loving your child, and then reach out to others around you who are hurting. This will lessen your heartache, and by reaching outward, you will find much inner healing flowing back into you.

Dear friend, partner in Christ, survivor (and winner)—as we complete our Year of Recovery, God's fresh elastic is gathering you and your family to him. Joy has been infused in you. He is in control, and maturity will come in His time—not yours—both to you and your child. Be patient, be faithful, and become a treasure in His Eternal Kingdom.

> Don't let the world around you squeeze you into its own mould, but let God re-mould your minds from within, so that you may prove in practice that the Plan of God for you is good, meets all His demands and moves toward the goal of true maturity.
>
> ROMANS 12:2 PHILLIPS

Fresh Elastic Survival Diploma

This is to certify that _____ has successfully completed the book FRESH ELASTIC FOR STRETCHED OUT MOMS and is on the journey to becoming a survivor. This achievement will become more visible as the *spring* comes back in her step, as her thoughts begin to *gather* more, and a smile will *snap* easily on her face. The fresh elastic is working. She is being made new!

Barbara Johnson

BARBARA JOHNSON

Humorist **Barbara Johnson** has sold more than five million books, including *Plant a Geranium in Your Cranium,* *Living Somewhere Between Estrogen and Death,* and *Stick a Geranium in Your Hat and Be Happy.* Founder of the nonprofit Spatula Ministries, she delivers comforting, humor-filled messages across the country as a popular conference speaker and part of the "Women of Faith" tour. She and her husband live in LaHabra, California.